D1217052

Visual Guide to

Financial Markets

How to Use This Book

The Bloomberg Financial Series is meant to serve as the all-encompassing, yet easy-to-follow, guide on today's most relevant finance and trading topics. The content lives up to the title by being visual; all charts are in color and presented in a large format for ease of use and readability. Other visual attributes include consistent elements that function as additional learning aids for the reader:

- Key Point sections: Primary ideas and takeaways, designed to help the reader skim through definitions and text.

- Definitions: Terminology and technical concepts that arise in the discussion.

- Step-by-Step instructions: Tutorials designed to ensure that readers understand and can execute each section of a multi-phase process.

- Do It Yourself: Worksheets, formulas, and calculations.

- Bloomberg Functionality Cheat Sheet: For Bloomberg terminal users, a back-of-the-book summary of relevant functions for the topics and tools discussed.

For e-reader users, *The Bloomberg Financial Series* is available as an enhanced e-book and offers special features, like an interactive Test Yourself section where readers can test their newly honed knowledge and skills. The enhanced e-book version includes video tutorials and special pop-up features. It can be purchased wherever e-books are sold.

Visual Guide to

Financial Markets

David Wilson

BLOOMBERG PRESS
An Imprint of

Published by John Wiley & Sons, Inc., Hoboken, New Jersey.

Published simultaneously in Canada.

For general information on our other products and services or for technical support, please contact our Customer Care Department within the United States at (800) 762-2974, outside the United States at (317) 572-3993 or fax (317) 572-4002.

Wiley also publishes its books in a variety of electronic formats. Some content that appears in print may not be available in electronic books. For more information about Wiley products, visit our web site at www.wiley.com.

Library of Congress Cataloging-in-Publication Data

Wilson, David, 1958 Mar. 28-
   Bloomberg visual guide to financial markets / David Wilson.
     p. cm. – (Bloomberg visual guide series)
   Includes bibliographical references and index.
   ISBN 978-1-118-20423-8 (pbk.); ISBN 978-1-118-22846-3 (ebk); ISBN 978-1-118-23325-2 (ebk); ISBN 978-1-118-26559-8 (ebk); ISBN 978-1-118-37348-4 (ebk); ISBN 978-1-118-37349-1 (ebk); ISBN 978-1-118-37350-7 (ebk)
   1. Finance.   2. Capital market.   3. Investments.   I. Title.
   HG173.W495 2012
   332′.0415 -dc23   2012001524

Printed in the United States of America

10 9 8 7 6 5 4 3 2 1

MIX
Paper from responsible sources
FSC
www.fsc.org
FSC® C101537

To Sandy,
who has taught me far more about life and love
than I ever taught her about business and finance.

Contents

Acknowledgments

This book is the product of more than two decades spent learning about and teaching financial markets at Bloomberg News even though it was put together in far less time.

Bloomberg's editor-in-chief, Matt Winkler, brought me on board in October 1990. Less than a year later, he and I started training 25 newly hired reporters for our Princeton, New Jersey, bureau. We spent eight weeks in a room with folding tables, bare floors, and air-conditioning ducts hanging from the ceiling.

Matt sent me to London the next year to run our first European training class, which meant getting my first passport. It was a thrill to teach currencies on the same day that George Soros became the man who broke the Bank of England, thanks to his hedge fund's billion-dollar bet against the British pound.

After serving as the bureau chief in Princeton and then in New York, I became Bloomberg News's first global training editor in 1994. For the next five years, I traveled the world to teach new reporters and editors about financial markets, journalism, and the Bloom-berg terminal. The position was an invaluable learning experience.

Some of the materials I put together during the period provided a foundation for this book. Handouts broke down quotes on securities and commodities in detail, and you'll find similar dissections in most of the chapters. Another handout highlighted what you'll come to know as the three Rs of financial markets: returns, risks, and relative value.

The training instinct came flooding back when my wife and I saw an off-off-Broadway play written by Ken Jaworowski, a former colleague, in October 2010. The characters included an economics professor who lectured his students about how the yield curve affected the outlook for growth. Afterward, I met the actor who played the professor and gave him an impromptu session on the topic, with curves drawn on the back of a paper placemat. Thanks, K.J., for the moment.

Matt suggested me as the author of this book, and I thank him and his chief of staff, Reto Gregori, for giving me the opportunity. I'm thankful to Stephen Isaacs, an editor-at-large at Bloomberg Press, and to

Evan Burton, Judy Howarth, and Chris Gage, my editors at John Wiley & Sons.

Chris Nagi and Nick Baker, who oversee my Chart of the Day stories for Bloomberg News, let me take time off as necessary to put the book together. I'm grateful to them, along with Al Mayers and Anthony Mancini at Bloomberg Radio, where I serve as stocks editor, for their support.

Brendan Moynihan and Shin Pei, editors-at-large for Bloomberg News, read this book in draft form and provided feedback that helped me improve the finished product. I appreciate their assistance.

I have worked with and trained many other people at Bloomberg News who deserve thanks. It would take pages to identify them all, so I hope they will accept my heartfelt gratitude as a group.

My goal as a financial journalist has been to tell stories in a way that my father, William, and my mother, Evelyn, could understand. Though neither of them worked in finance, they followed the subject as it related to our family. They both have passed away, and I carry their memory with me always.

The comments of a couple of friends, Runi Sriwardena and Robin Vitale, reinforced the need to keep things as simple as possible. I'm grateful to them for the reminder, and I did the best I could to meet that goal.

Finally, I'd like to thank my wife, Sandy, for her love and friendship over the years. Little did she know when we first met in the mid-1990s at Bloomberg News that she would end up married to an author. Then again, I didn't know anyone who shared my attitude toward life until she came along.

While I was working on the book, Sandy's efforts allowed me to come home and focus on my "night job" after putting in a full day at the office. I'm grateful for her willingness to let me pursue this, and I hope the results are worth the sacrifice.

David Wilson, February 2012

Introduction

Financial markets are supposed to be complicated. If they were easier to understand, there wouldn't be as much money to go around. Individual investors wouldn't need to pay brokers and financial advisers as much to manage their nest eggs. They might be less inclined to buy high and sell low, ensuring profits for those who do the opposite.

This book is designed to make things simpler. It's built around the choices that you have about where to put your money, an approach that's more in keeping with the investment decisions that people make in the real world.

Look at it this way: If a family member asked you for some money to start a business, your first thought probably wouldn't be about the kind of securities you would receive in return. More than likely, it would be about the person, his or her relationship to you, success in life and work, background in business, and any past requests made for financial help.

You'll find three basic equivalents of the family member in financial markets:

1. Governments, which rely on money from investors to bridge gaps between spending and taxes. The bigger the budget deficit, the more borrowing they need to do.

2. Companies, which raise funds to run and expand their business and enable owners to buy and sell their investments.

3. Hard assets, which have a presence that goes beyond entries in computer databases or on scraps of paper. Gold is one example that many investors favor. Commodities and real estate are others.

After deciding what to invest in, you have to figure out how to put your money to work. You can invest directly in governments, companies, and hard assets, and there's more than one choice for each. You can make investments that indirectly reflect their value as well.

Chapter 1 provides an overview of direct investing and introduces a format used throughout the book. We'll begin with the basics, especially the assets and the markets where they are bought and sold. After that, we'll dissect a market quotation as it might appear on a Bloomberg terminal.

We'll conclude with a review of the three Rs of financial markets: returns, risks, and relative value. We'll go through the components of returns, including interest on bonds and dividends on stocks. We'll examine the risks that can reduce those returns. Finally, we'll look at ways that investors determine whether an asset is cheap, expensive, or fairly valued.

Government markets are our next stop in Chapter 2. We'll start by determining why you're effectively making an investment in the government when keeping cash in a bank account or maybe under a mattress. The answer lies in currencies.

We'll look at lending money to the government. You have a choice between buying bills, IOUs that pay off in no more than a year; notes, which last for as long as 10 years; and bonds, which raise funds for longer periods. We'll tackle bills before moving into notes and bonds.

Companies compete with the government to raise money in financial markets, and Chapter 3 spells out how. They can raise funds for a year or less by selling securities that are similar to government bills. To line up financing for longer periods, they can turn to notes and bonds instead.

Another choice for companies isn't available to governments: selling partial ownership, otherwise known as equity. This chapter explains how investors can distinguish one company's shares from another's.

Hard assets are an alternative to stocks, bonds, and cash, and Chapters 4 is all about them. Gold comes first because many investors consider the precious metal to be separate from other assets. Then we'll look at commodities and real estate.

Indexes enable investors to track how well or poorly financial markets are performing. These indicators provide a way for them to assess their own performance, or those of the managers working for them. They provide a way to invest as well because many index-based funds are available. Chapter 5 presents indexes that are based on direct investments.

Chapters 6 through 8 revisit government, companies, and hard assets to introduce additional markets. Government debt includes state and local borrowing, along with many bonds backed by home mortgages. Companies sell securities that are a cross between bonds and stocks, and take out bank loans. Investors can profit from hard assets without having to own them, and we'll look at commodity and real estate businesses that provide an added bonus of tax benefits.

The remainder of the book explores indirect investing, or markets that are one step removed from ownership of government IOUs, corporate securities, and hard assets. Chapter 9 provides an overview of the two main categories for this type of investing, derivatives and funds.

Derivatives are covered in more detail in Chapter 10. The value of these contracts is tied to some other investment, such as a stock, a bond, an interest rate, a currency, or an index. We'll review three basic types—futures, options, and swaps—and touch on a few variations as well.

Chapter 11 is all about funds. Their value is based on investments made by someone else, namely the manager. We'll go through mutual funds and exchange-traded funds, or ETFs, along with alternative funds for wealthier investors that are more complex and costly.

The final chapter revisits the subject of indexes. We'll look at indicators based on derivatives and funds, and we'll learn what investors do with them.

That's a lot to go through, and each chapter could be developed as its own book. Even so, you'll be able to gain a basic knowledge of financial markets by the time you're done. Charts and visual aids show what each chapter is telling.

With all that in mind, let's get started.

DIRECT INVESTING

IBM 1.95 07/16 $ ↓ **103.373 -.137**
At 09:47 Vol 2,000 Op 103.373 Hi 103.373 Lo 103.373 YLD 1.153 TRAC

Exhibit 1.2: An IBM Bond Quote

for International Business Machines Corp., differs from what you see in Exhibit 1.2, a quote for one of IBM's bonds.

Yet some facts and figures are usually included, no matter what the security, and they are worth knowing now. Let's take a closer look at them.

Security symbol: This code, known as **a ticker,** is the first thing you'll see in any quote. Some symbols identify only the original seller or the issuer. Others include details about the security itself.

Uptick/downtick arrow: The direction of the arrow shows the last change, usually in the price. It's known as an uptick/downtick arrow because each price move in a security is called a tick. ▲▼

Latest price: This is the most basic piece of data in any quote. It's usually taken from trades. Some investments aren't quoted at a price as we'll see later.

Change on the day: By comparing this figure with the latest price, you'll know how much the market value has moved during the day.

Bid price: This is the highest price that anyone is willing to pay. It's shown because a seller would rather get as much money as possible, all other things being equal.

Ask price: This is the lowest price at which anyone is willing to sell. It's known as the offer price. By either name, it's the flip side of the bid price, as a buyer would rather pay as little as possible. The difference between the bid and ask prices is known as the bid-ask spread. The narrower the spread, the easier it is for investors to buy and sell without moving the price, and vice versa.

Time: This shows whether the latest price is a reasonable indication of market value. If it's a minute or two old, then the answer is probably yes. If it's an hour or two old, then maybe not. Times are presented in 24-hour format. This means that a stock price posted at the close of U.S. stock exchanges, 4 p.m. Eastern time, would appear as 16:00.

Price range: Opening, high, and low prices for the day's trading put the current price in context. How much have prices moved during the day? Is the current price closer to the high or the low? It's easier to answer these questions when the data are readily available. For the same reason, many quotes include the previous day's closing price.

STEP-BY-STEP:
REAL RETURN MATH

1. **The Standard & Poor's 500 Index fell 0.003 percent in 2011.**
2. **Dividends paid during the year equaled 2.089 percent of the index's value.**
3. **Add price changes and dividends to calculate the nominal return of 2.086 percent, or 2.1 percent after rounding.**
4. **Inflation was 3.4 percent, based on the change in the Consumer Price Index (CPI) for the 12 months ended in November.**
5. **Subtract inflation from the nominal return to calculate the real return of minus 1.3 percent.**

You may have noticed that volume, or the amount of trading, isn't part of this list. That's no accident. Volume is available mainly for stocks and other securities that trade on exchanges. For currencies, bonds, and hard assets, they often are hard to find or undisclosed.

Three Rs

Now that you have gone this far, it's time to address a basic question: What's in it for me? Put another way, how would markets for investing in governments, companies, and hard assets affect me? To find the answer, you have to focus on the three Rs of returns, risks, and relative value.

The first two Rs, returns and risks, go together. If one investment produces higher returns than another, then it's usually riskier as well. Investors who pay too much attention to the returns can end up suffering unexpected losses when a change in market direction highlights the risks.

Relative value, the third R, begins with understanding the relationship between the first two. If the price of a security or hard asset falls, it's possible the move might be temporary and the potential returns may rise accordingly. It's also possible the investment has become more speculative. Returns in the future may be the same or lower after adjusting for the added risk.

These kinds of judgments are essential in determining whether an investment is cheap, expensive, or fairly priced, the goal of relative-value analysis. They can be made for a specific security, between securi-

ties in a single market, between market segments, and among markets as we'll see again later.

Returns

Price changes usually make the biggest contribution to returns on an investment. Their effect depends on the direction of the move and on whether an investor owns the security or asset or is betting on a decline.

The first point is obvious enough. Investors in a government, company, or hard asset want to make money. The same goes for anyone who's betting against them. The second point refers to whether someone has a long or short position.

Investors can go long through the primary or secondary market. Either way, the price they pay for a security or asset becomes the starting point for determining their returns.

To go short, investors borrow securities or assets and sell them as mentioned earlier. The borrowing is usually conducted in a securities-lending market, where investors are paid for making their holdings available.

The price of the second transaction, or short sale, is the basis for calculating returns. If the price declines, then short sellers can make money by buying back whatever was sold and by repaying the lender. Their profit comes from the gap between the short sale and market prices. If the security or asset rises, then the short seller loses.

When we study returns later, we'll focus on what investors in governments, companies, and hard assets will earn. Remember, though, that rising prices don't lead to gains for everyone invested in a market. Lower prices don't hurt everyone either.

We'll consider what else affects returns besides changes in price. Anyone who lends money to governments and companies typically earns interest. Stocks often pay dividends. Gold and other commodities don't provide either type of payment, which means returns are more closely tied to price moves. Real estate owners receive lease payments or rental income.

Inflation reduces returns by making these payments less valuable before they are received. Investors take this effect into account by tracking real returns, which are adjusted for inflation. Figures that don't have any adjustment are known as nominal returns.

Costs and expenses hurt returns. Buying and selling securities and hard assets requires the payment of trading fees. Having someone hold them in an account adds to the cost. You incur storage and transportation expense for commodities and maintenance expenses for real estate. Taxes are imposed on interest and dividend payments and investment gains as a rule.

Because the costs can vary considerably from one investor to the next, we'll keep the discussion of them to a minimum in later chapters. Even so, you should learn about the tax benefits that go with investing in some markets.

Risks

Investors probably wouldn't bother putting money into governments, companies, and hard assets if they knew the prices of their holdings would fall

rather than rise. Yet that's a risk they inevitably take when they buy securities, commodities, or real estate.

The short sellers we encountered earlier have the opposite risk. When their asset's price increases, the value of their short position declines, and vice versa. Their losses can be infinite. Buyers can only lose what they paid for their holdings plus investment fees and expenses.

Either way, prices may go in the wrong direction. This is called market risk. It's a concern for anyone who's invested in a security or market, whether the holding is direct or indirect.

Another universal risk is the threat that investors won't be able to sell an asset at the current market price because there aren't enough potential buyers around. This is known as liquidity risk. The phrase refers to the ability to raise cash, known as a liquid asset. Some investments are more liquid than others because there's more trading in them. It's probably much easier to sell a 10-year Treasury note, for example, than a 10-year corporate note. That's the case because the government security changes hands all day, and the company debt might trade occasionally.

Demand for actively traded securities sometimes evaporates. Shares of some of the biggest U.S. companies changed hands for as little as one cent a share on May 6, 2010, when the Standard & Poor's 500 Index plunged as much as 10 percent before rebounding. That's liquidity risk in the extreme.

KEY POINT:

For owners of a security or hard asset, market risk is the possibility of a drop in value. For short sellers, it's the opposite.

DEFINITION:

Liquidity

Liquidity is the ease of buying and selling without causing price changes.

Risks found outside the markets can trip up investors in governments, companies, and hard assets as well. Four of them are worth a closer look.

We'll start with economic risk, or the possibility that slower growth or contraction—in the worst case, a recession or depression—will cut government tax revenue along with corporate sales and earnings. Risk exists when growth accelerates, as companies must pay more for workers or raw materials. Companies most vulnerable to this risk are known as cyclicals because their fortunes are closely linked to the economy's up-and-down cycles.

Political risk is the potential for legislative actions to deter or prevent governments and companies from reaching their goals. This risk was especially pronounced for the United States in July and August 2011 when President Barack Obama and Congress were unable to agree on raising the country's debt ceiling until the limit was almost reached.

Policy risk is a specific type of political risk, which isn't limited to the executive and legislative branches. It's focused on monetary policy, controlled by the Federal Reserve (Fed) and other central banks, and fiscal policy, defined by taxing and spending decisions made by the president and Congress.

Monetary policy affects the amount of funds available to the economy as well as their cost, otherwise known as interest rates. The Fed's version is designed to meet two goals: containing inflation and maximizing employment. The central bank pursues these objectives by adjusting the amount of money in the economy from day to day and by setting benchmark rates.

Additional moves are made when necessary, as they were during the 2008 financial crisis and its aftermath. The Fed added hundreds of billions of dollars to the economy through bond purchases, a practice known as quantitative easing, and started paying interest on funds that banks kept on deposit.

Fiscal policy shapes the way a government takes in and spends money, which in turn affects the economy's performance. The types of taxes that households and businesses must pay and the rates they are charged affect the revenue side. Outlays are linked to decisions about national defense, social programs, and other areas that the government manages.

Policy decisions can explain why the U.S. federal budget was balanced for part of the 1990s, for instance. They can account for the deficits that reached more than $1 trillion annually during the next decade.

Investors have to concern themselves with currency risk. Because U.S. stocks and bonds are priced in dollars, their value is affected by the dollar's value against other currencies. If the dollar is dropping, then demand from non-U.S. investors may decline, causing prices to fall.

Currency risk can cut the opposite way as well. A rising dollar makes U.S. exports more costly to overseas buyers, which tends to reduce international trade and curtail economic growth. Gains in the dollar reduce the value of sales and profits that U.S. companies make outside the country.

KEY POINT:

Currency-market moves can affect the value of any investment. When the dollar is rising, demand for investments priced in the U.S. currency tends to increase. When the dollar is falling, assets denominated in other currencies become more valuable.

We'll examine more specific risks in later chapters. Credit risk, or the ability of a government or company to keep up payments on its debt, is one of them. Another is business risk, or the threat that a company's operations or finances may falter.

Relative Value

U.S. government bills, maturing in one year or less, paid next to nothing after the Fed began targeting near-zero interest rates at the end of 2008. Earlier in the 2000s, the securities rewarded investors with rates of 6 percent or more. During the 1980s, rates exceeded 10 percent.

The historical comparisons show Treasury debt is far less lucrative than it used to be. They provide a starting point for determining whether the securities are cheap, expensive, or fairly priced in relative terms. Similar analysis is done on all the other types of securities we'll cover.

History only tells part of the story. Investors have to determine how much risk there is today for a government, company, or hard asset. Then they have to decide whether the potential returns are high enough to justify taking that risk.

The opinions of credit-rating services, especially Standard & Poor's, Moody's Investors Service, and Fitch Ratings, are often part of that process. These companies assess the risks that go with debt securities. Their judgments help shape the views of investors, for better or worse.

Investors may study two securities that are essentially the same except for the maturity date or another key detail. Relative-value analysis would help them decide whether the difference matters, based on the potential returns.

The same issue arises when looking at similar securities from different entities. Suppose investors can choose between a three-month government bill and a corporate security maturing at about the same time. The company probably will be a riskier bet than the government. If the corporate security provides enough additional income to compensate for the greater risk, it may be worth buying. If not, it's the other way around.

Different securities from the same entity can be studied this way. Consider the example of a company that has publicly traded bonds and shares. It's possible to decide which is cheaper by comparing interest payments on the debt with dividends on the stock even though the payments aren't identical.

Relative-value comparisons like these can be extended to entire markets. They help investors decide whether to focus on stocks or bonds, how much cash to keep on hand, and whether to put money into hard assets, among other things.

The criteria used to determine what's cheap, expensive, and fairly priced vary by market. For bills, notes, bonds, and other types of debt, interest rates are important. Though the rates differ, as we'll learn later, there's a common thread to how they are interpreted. Investors want to know how much they stand to earn for lending out money, and rates are the guidepost.

STEP-BY-STEP: RISK AND RETURN

1. Suppose a three-month Treasury bill has a 0.1 percent rate.
2. Suppose a three-month corporate security has a 0.5 percent rate.
3. Subtract the Treasury bill rate from the corporate rate, and what's left is 0.4 percent.
4. The 0.4 percent is what an investor gets paid for lending money to the company, rather than the government.
5. The investor has to determine whether the additional amount is worth the risk.
6. Relative-value analysis guides the decision-making.

Investors in debt securities are concerned with a borrower's ability to pay interest on time and repay the money when it's due. This leads them to focus on cash: where it's coming from, where it's going, how much exists, and how fast it's growing. The less a borrower needs the money, the more secure someone will be with owning its debt.

Stock investors also concentrate on cash. For one thing, they're interested in a company's ability to pay dividends. For another, companies with cash can buy back shares, which can increase returns on the remaining stock. These payouts help determine relative value as do revenue and earnings, which indicate how well the business is doing.

Relative-value comparisons are more basic for hard assets, if only because less data are available. For commodities, history and supply-demand analysis play larger roles than they would in securities. There aren't any interest, dividends, and earnings to use in deciding what's cheap and expensive.

In real estate, it's possible to assess value through comparisons between a property and similar ones that have been sold recently. That said, the analysis isn't as straightforward as finding rates on bonds or financial ratios for stocks. Real estate doesn't change hands that often, so the right numbers can be elusive.

CHAPTER 2

Government

Can you imagine an investment that carries no risk? No worries about markets, liquidity, or anything else? What kind of an interest rate would you expect this investment to provide? Put another way, what kind of a return would you need to be a buyer?

For many investors, the answer to the first two questions is "yes." That's because a risk-free rate is often used in evaluating returns and in making relative-value judgments. The rate is theoretical because every investment carries some risk.

The third and fourth questions can be answered by looking at the interest rate on three-month Treasury bills. It's reasonably close to a risk-free U.S. rate for a couple of reasons. First, the government can require many of the more than 300 million Americans to pay taxes, and the revenue is a source of funds for making payments on the securities. Second, the government has the ability to pay with new money.

Other borrowers don't have the two advantages working for them. This means government securities markets are a relatively sure bet for investors. The three-month period provides an additional margin of safety as there isn't much time for risks to surface. The promise to pay goes with bills, a form of debt. The government can't sell equity, a riskier type of investment.

Some safety exists in cash, as suggested by the image of people stuffing their money under a mattress during times of economic turmoil. Government is responsible for sustaining the value of that cash as it makes decisions on a country's borrowing.

Remember, though, that risk-free remains a relative term. Government debt can lose value as interest rates rise and inflation accelerates, as do other securities. Investors who turn over their money for longer periods can suffer bigger losses when rates or inflation go against them. We'll explore the risks later in this chapter. For now, let's take a closer look at currencies.

> **KEY POINT:**
> Rates on government securities are sometimes called risk-free rates because the debt carries little risk for investors.

Currencies

We often measure the value of money by how far it goes at the supermarket, the shopping mall, the online store, and other retail locations. Another barometer serves as the foundation for a multitrillion-dollar market: the amount of a foreign currency we can purchase.

Money comes in pairs in the foreign exchange markets. Pairs that include the dollar tend to be watched most closely. The dollar is a reserve currency, held by central banks and used internationally to set the price of goods and services. Because the United States is the world's largest economy, there are plenty of dollars crossing borders each day.

Each pair has two values, based on buying or selling one unit of the currency. There's a value, for instance, that shows Japanese tourists en route to the United States how many dollars they can buy with their yen. Another exists for the U.S. businessman going to Tokyo, who has the opposite concern. The values are mirror images of each other, as shown in Exhibit 2.1.

Only one of the values in any currency pair is front and center on traders' computer screens. Usually, it's the amount of another currency you can buy for a dollar. That's the case with the yen.

There are prominent exceptions. The euro, Europe's common currency, is among them. Traders focus on the number of dollars and cents required to buy one euro and not the reverse. Others include British Commonwealth currencies, especially the British pound and the Australian and New Zealand dollars.

Currency pairs that exclude the dollar get some attention. Their exchange rates are called cross rates because they reflect each currency's value against the dollar. This assumes someone will go across the dollar—buying dollars with one currency and selling those dollars for the other currency—to complete a trade. If the dollar trades at 80 yen and the pound is at $1.60, the pound-yen cross rate is 80 times 1.60, or 128 yen to the pound.

Regardless of the pairing, currency moves can affect economies and financial markets. A declining currency makes a country's goods and services cheaper in international markets, and vice versa. This may encourage more people to visit, like those Japanese tourists, and to invest in government securities, companies, and hard assets.

Foreign exchange swings can be a double benefit or a double whammy for investment returns. If a stock or bond rises, a strengthening of the currency in which it's denominated will enhance the gain. If the price drops, a weaker currency will magnify the loss.

Trillions of dollars changes hands daily in the global currency markets. The latest available figure is $4 trillion, taken from an April 2010 survey by the Bank for International Settlements (BIS). The BIS, which assists central banks and monetary authorities worldwide, canvasses them every three years on trading in currencies and related contracts.

STEP-BY-STEP: FROM DOLLARS TO YEN

1. Assume the dollar is trading at 80 yen.
2. The yen's value is the inverse, so divide 80 by 100.
3. One yen is equal to 80/100 of a dollar, or 0.8 cent.

STEP-BY-STEP: FROM POUNDS TO DOLLARS

1. Assume the pound is trading at $1.60.
2. The dollar's value is the inverse, so divide 100 by 1.60.
3. One dollar is equal to 100/1.60, or 62.5 pence.

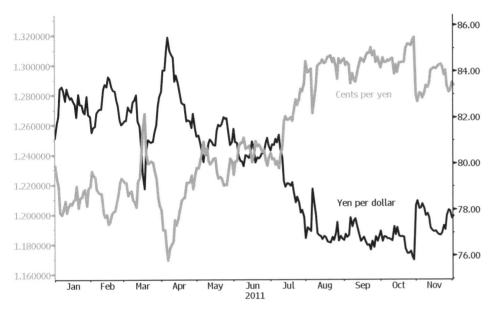

Exhibit 2.1: Dollar's Value in Yen and Yen's Value in Dollars

Practically all this buying and selling takes place over the counter, or away from exchanges. Banks, brokers, and other financial companies connect over electronic networks to carry out their trading. This approach means the amount of information available about foreign exchange trading from day to day is relatively sparse, as we'll see shortly.

Quotations

Suppose you were that businessman who traveled to Tokyo from New York and needed to exchange currency. You could go to an automated teller machine (ATM) and withdraw the number of yen you wanted. You may stop at a bank branch, a foreign-exchange kiosk at the airport, or a hotel's front desk.

If you choose one of these other locations, you'll run across a table with three columns. The first has the names of currencies, including the dollar. The second shows how much you would receive in return for each currency, and the third shows how much you would have to pay to buy them. The line for the dollar might look like this: **JPY 76.25 78.75**.

The first number is the bid price, and the second is the ask, or offer, price. The gap between them, 2.5 yen, is the bid-ask spread. The wider the spread, the greater the profits for a bank, money changer, or hotel from currency exchange.

Bid and ask prices are all that are disclosed in the global foreign exchange market. Prices at which currencies trade aren't made public, which means there's little detail available to show in quotes. Take the Japanese yen as an example (see Exhibit 2.2).

There's no way to tell how many yen changed hands during the day, or the exact price at which dollars were sold for yen. Let's find out what is available.

JPY: The quote's first line begins with a three-letter code for the yen. Each currency has a code. Some of the more popular ones are EUR for the euro, GBP for the British pound, CAD for the Canadian dollar, and CHF for the Swiss franc. When only three letters are included, the other currency is the dollar. Six-letter codes are used for cross rates, where the dollar isn't involved in the trade. EURJPY, for example, shows the value of one euro in yen.

76.33: This is the number of yen one dollar will buy. It's known as the **mid price** because it's halfway between the bid and ask prices.

−.13: Change from the previous day's last price, recorded at 5 p.m. New York time in this case. Currency markets don't open and close during the week, as trading happens worldwide 24 hours a day. The last price might be based on trading in London, home to the world's biggest foreign exchange market, or in Tokyo, another currency trading hub, for some market participants.

BGN 76.32/76.33 BGN: Highest bid and lowest ask prices, along with the source of each. BGN stands for Bloomberg generic pricing, which combines quotes from a number of banks. In other cases, a code for a specific bank may appear.

The spread between them is 0.01 yen, far narrower than the 2.5-yen differential in our earlier example. That's the case because there's far more currency bought and sold in the market than at bank branches, currency kiosks, and hotels.

At 14:32: The second line begins with the time at which the mid price was recorded. This is as common as the uptick/downtick arrow in quotes, as you'll see later. It's essential because currency values, like security prices, are constantly changing.

Op 76.46: Opening price, recorded shortly after 5 p.m. New York time the day before.

```
JPY      76.33    -.13 BGN  76.32/76.33 BGN
At 14:32 Op 76.46 Hi 76.97 Lo 76.11 Close 76.46
```

Exhibit 2.2: Yen Quote

Hi 76.97: High price for the current trading day.

Lo 76.11: Low price for the current trading day.

Close 76.46: Closing price for the previous day. It's the basis for the day's change of –.13, shown in the first line.

Three Rs

The Japanese tourists and the U.S. businessman introduced earlier are exchanging currency to cover expenses rather than to turn a profit. The same might be said about companies doing business internationally. They may need to buy another currency to complete a purchase or to make an exchange for their local currency to bring revenue home.

Many investors make foreign exchange trades for similar reasons. Funds that invest outside their home country need the local currency to purchase stocks, bonds, and other assets. Some of these funds trade to reduce the risk that currency moves will affect their profits.

Currency speculators have another goal in mind. They want to make money as one currency rises or falls in value against another. We'll look at the three Rs of returns, risks, and relative value from their perspective.

Returns

Speculators buy and sell currencies in anticipation of changes in exchange rates over time. Returns from making these bets depend on how rates move. The potential for swings reflects the willingness of governments to allow markets to set the value of their currencies.

Some rates are fixed, which means they don't move. Argentina, for example, set the value of its peso at $1 between 1991 and 2002. The fixing of the exchange rate helped the country bounce back from years of economic contraction.

Fixed exchange rates are an example of pegging, known as linking, in which governments determine the value of currencies. In other cases, monetary authorities set the range in which the value can fluctuate and buy and sell currency to maintain the range. In 2005, Hong Kong pegged its dollar at HK$7.75 to HK$7.85 to the U.S. dollar and China let its currency—the renminbi, denominated in yuan—float within a band tied to a basket of currencies.

Then there are the freely floating currencies, where the value is almost entirely determined in markets. The "almost" is included because central banks occasionally stage what's known as an intervention. They buy and sell currencies when values get too far out of line for their liking.

Central banks can set lower exchange rates through currency devaluations. The dollar was last devalued in 1934, when the amount of gold that the U.S. currency could buy was cut by 41 percent. The pound's value tumbled 4 percent on Sept. 16, 1992, when the United Kingdom withdrew from an agreement that fixed its exchange rate. Several emerging market currencies have been devalued more recently.

DEFINITION:
Speculators

Speculators buy and sell to profit from changes in market value.

Generally, the daily movements in floating currencies—the dollar, euro, yen, British pound and Swiss franc, to name a few—reflect what tourists, businessmen, companies, speculators, and others are buying and selling. This means they provide the greatest potential for returns.

Exchange rate changes aren't entirely tied to returns though. Speculators don't buy currencies and hide them under a mattress or in a corner office. Instead, they deposit the funds in a bank and earn interest.

Banks dominate currency trading worldwide, so it makes sense that they would end up with the money. Deposits are the investment of choice because their market and liquidity risk is low. This reduces the odds of investment losses that would cut into returns if the currency moves the right way.

Put this all together, and it's understandable that deposit rates would affect the flow of funds into and out of currencies, as well as their returns. Money tends to flow into a country as rates increase and flow out as rates fall.

Banks take their lead on what to pay for deposits from a central bank, such as the Fed. They're guided by a rate that the central bank sets directly. The United States has a target rate for overnight loans between banks that's known as the federal funds rate. The Fed's policy makers set the target, and the central bank adjusts the amount of money in the banking system each business day to control the market rate.

Speculators can deposit funds in the country that printed the money or elsewhere. Interest rates for deposits made outside the country are known as Eurodollar rates. Although the name originally referred to European bank deposits of dollars, the Euro-prefix has come to mean foreign. There are Eurodollar rates in Tokyo and Euroyen rates outside of Japan.

Risks

We've seen how market and liquidity risks affect the currency market. Anyone buying stocks, bonds, or hard assets with their money, rather than depositing the funds in a bank, is more likely to sustain losses. They may be large enough to wipe out any gains from exchange-rate moves.

Political, economic, and policy risks are part of the territory as well. After all, U.S. paper money says "The United States of America" and "Federal Reserve Note." This means the president, Congress, and the Fed each has a role to play in determining its value.

Market-specific issues also exist, beginning with interest rate risk. Because money obtained through the currency market goes into bank deposits, the rate is set for a certain period. If the central bank raises rates during that time, the deposit won't earn as much money as it might have otherwise. Currency moves tied to the rate increase may not make up for this lost opportunity.

Inflation risk is another concern. When prices are rising, the money on a deposit will buy less than it might have otherwise. If the inflation rate exceeds the deposit rate, the funds will buy less. Put another way, inflation reduces the purchasing power of money, whether it's in your wallet, your pocketbook, or a bank.

In extreme cases, inflation turns into hyperinflation. Prices rise so far and fast that the increases essentially wipe out a currency's value. This took place in Germany after World War I and in several emerging markets more recently.

The African country of Zimbabwe provided a worst-case scenario during the 2000s, as shown in Exhibit 2.3. Soaring prices prompted Zimbabwe's central bank to redenominate its currency, the dollar, multiple times. The central bank resorted to printing bills with face values as high as Z$100 trillion before doing away with the local currency in 2009.

Relative Value

What does the same item cost in different locations? The answer provides a way to determine the value of one currency against another. McDonald's Big Mac sandwiches and Starbucks lattes have been used in these kinds of comparisons because they're so widely available.

The analysis is based on the principle that people should be able to buy goods and services for the same price anywhere. Economists refer to this as purchasing power parity. Ideally, exchange rates would maintain parity, though it doesn't quite work out that way in currency markets.

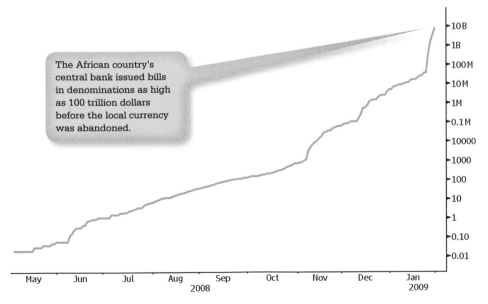

The African country's central bank issued bills in denominations as high as 100 trillion dollars before the local currency was abandoned.

Exhibit 2.3: Number of Zimbabwe Dollars per U.S. Dollar During Hyperinflation

DEFINITION:
Treasury bills

Treasury bills are securities that the U.S. government sells to borrow funds for a year or less. Investors and companies classify them as cash equivalents.

There's another relative-value gauge that was mentioned earlier: deposit rates. The gap in rates between two countries influences the movement of money between them, which in turn affects exchange rates. For currency speculators, the rate differential counts for more than Big Macs and lattes.

Bills

Trillion-dollar budget gaps have to be closed somehow. The U.S. government has learned this lesson the hard way in the past few years. Increased spending to help sustain the country's economy and fluctuations in tax revenue swelled the federal deficit to more than $1 trillion annually.

Investors made up the shortfall. The government stepped up fundraising in the money market, where money is made available for as long as a year. It leaned more heavily on the bond market to borrow for two to 30 years.

We'll visit the government bond market shortly, so let's focus on the money market. The U.S. Treasury sells debt securities maturing in one, three, six, or 12 months on a regular schedule, and for other periods as needed. They are known as Treasury bills.

The word "bills" may make you think about the $1, $5, $10, and $20 bills in your wallet or pocketbook. That's an idea worth keeping in mind. Treasury bills play much the same role as paper money even though the government doesn't print and distribute them. Accountants consider them the same as cash, like other money market securities we'll run across later. Companies refer to them as cash equivalents in financial statements.

Treasury bills are as safe an investment as you'll find in financial markets, for a couple of reasons. First, consider the government's power to impose taxes on tens of millions of people and millions of companies to pay its debts. No other borrower is in that position. Second, the government can create money through the central bank. If worse came to worst, it would be possible to obtain the money by cranking up the Fed's printing presses. That's an option no one else has.

The relative safety of government bills is tied to their maturity date. There's less potential for things to go wrong in a year than there is in five, 10, or 30 years. What might happen? We'll find out when we examine the three Rs.

Investors can buy bills in the primary or secondary market. The primary market consists of auctions conducted by the Federal Reserve Bank of New York (New York Fed) on the Treasury's behalf. The secondary market is run by the largest banks and securities firms, along with the brokers that connect them.

The Treasury currently sells one-month, three-month, and six-month bills each week, along with one-year bills each month. Some banks and securities firms are required to bid at every auction, ensuring the government will have buyers for whatever bills are sold. These bidders are known as primary dealers, a title that fits their position within the primary market.

Primary dealers compete at auctions by submitting bids, based on the interest rate they're willing to accept.

The New York Fed then sells the bills at the lowest possible rate, which translates into the highest price. This enables the Treasury to borrow as cheaply as possible.

Investors can buy new bills through primary dealers or straight from the Treasury. If they go through a dealer, the firm's auction bid will largely determine what they have to pay. They can go through Treasury Direct, a program that lets smaller investors buy securities at the average rates set in auctions.

These rates are known as discount rates because Treasury bills are bought for less than their face value.

The securities don't pay interest before they mature, so the size of the discount has much to do with their returns, the first of the three Rs. They are stated as annual rates for consistency's sake even for bills maturing in less than a year, as most of them do.

As 2008 ended, discount rates at bill auctions dropped to almost zero. The decline resulted from the Fed's efforts to prop up the U.S. economy through monetary policy. Put another way, the government could pay almost nothing to borrow money. Exhibit 2.4 places the borrowing costs in perspective.

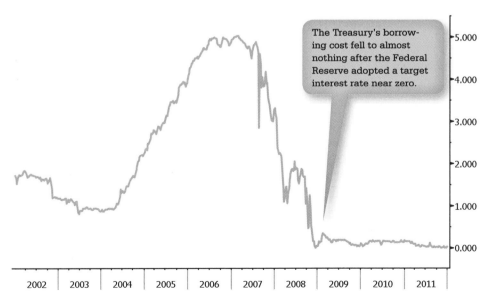

The Treasury's borrowing cost fell to almost nothing after the Federal Reserve adopted a target interest rate near zero.

Exhibit 2.4: Three-Month Treasury Bill's High Discount Rate at Auction
Sources: U.S. Treasury, Bloomberg.

Discount rates are the focus in the secondary market, where the primary dealers and others trade bills sold at past auctions. There isn't an exchange where the securities are bought and sold. Instead, trades are made between firms electronically in the over-the-counter (OTC) market.

Securities firms operate their own electronic trading networks. Similar systems are provided by independent firms, including Bloomberg, which has one called Bloomberg BondTrader for Treasury bills and other debt securities.

Dealers may use brokers to carry out trades. Cantor Fitzgerald LP, ICAP Plc, and Tullett Prebon Plc operate three of the biggest brokerages for bills and other government securities, including the notes and bonds we'll study later in this chapter.

Quotations

Prices are nowhere to be found in quotes on Treasury bills. Instead, they are quoted at discount rates, in keeping with how they're sold at auctions. This rate determines the price that a buyer will pay.

The number or dollar amount of bills traded during the day won't be found in quotes either. They're omitted because the OTC markets where they trade don't make the data widely available.

Now that we know what isn't in Treasury bill quotes, let's look at what is (see Exhibit 2.5).

B: Symbol for Treasury bills.

9/20/12: Maturity date, when the holder receives face value from the Treasury. It's shown in month/day/year format.

Up arrow: Direction of the most recent change in the discount rate. Because the rate moved up, this is known as an uptick. A down arrow would signify a decline in the rate, or a downtick. You'll see arrows like this in many other quotes.

This uptick/downtick arrow tracks the discount rate rather than the price. Higher rates mean lower prices, and vice versa. Keep that in mind, as it's true for other types of debt securities.

.090: Discount rate in percentage points. Investors buying this bill would earn 0.09 point on their investment by keeping it until the maturity date. That amounts to nine cents for every $1,000 invested. Percentages like this are so small that traders and investors move the decimal point two places to the right and talk about basis points. Each basis point amounts to 0.01 percentage point, so the bill's discount rate is 9 basis points.

DEFINITION:
Basis points

Basis points are hundredths of a percentage point

▲ B 09/20/12 ↑ **.090** − **.005** .095/.090
▼ At 14:33 Op .095 Hi .100 Lo .080 Prev .095 CBBT

Exhibit 2.5: A Treasury Bill Quote

.005: Today's rate change in percentage points. For the bill, it's 0.005 point. We might as well move the decimal point again and refer to the drop as half a basis point.

.095/.090: Bid and ask rates. The bid rate is higher because the resulting price will be lower. For the ask rate, it's the other way around.

At 14:33: Time of the quote, using the 24-hour clock.

Op .095, Hi .100, Lo .080, Prev .095: Opening, high, and low rates for the current day and closing rate for the previous day.

CBBT: Source of the current rate. This is a composite quote from Bloomberg BondTrader.

Three Rs

Safety comes with a price in the government bill market. It's measured by the potential return, which usually won't come close to matching what's available on other investments. On the other hand, the risks are relatively low as well. The United States has paid its debts on time for decades and isn't poised to follow companies and some local governments into bankruptcy court.

The relative safety explains why the rate the United States pays to borrow has historically been known as a risk-free rate. The phrase isn't quite accurate, as noted earlier, because investors face risks even when the government's finances are sound. We'll explore them as we go through the three Rs, and learn how investors find relative value.

Returns

Because government bills don't pay interest before maturity, their returns depend mainly on the difference between the purchase price and face value. The price, in turn, results from the quoted discount rate.

As an example, let's assume you bought Treasury bills maturing in one year at a 0.1 percent rate. Based on how the math works out, you would pay about $999 for every $1,000 face amount of the securities.

These bills are bound to rise in value as the number of days to maturity, or the amount of time until that final $1,000 payment is due, gets smaller. Changes in market rates will affect how and when the increase occurs. In the end, the price will equal $1,000 as long as the Treasury is paying its debts on time.

Risks

Bills are a type of fixed-income security, as the timing and amount of the payment are preset. Investors in the securities are taking the same kinds of risks as they do with government bonds, corporate debt, and related securities as we'll see later.

The most basic concern is whether a borrower, in this instance the government, will be able to pay on time. This is known as credit risk. The discount rate is a gauge of the amount of risk that investors see. The higher the rate, the greater the concern, and vice versa. Bond yields, which we'll learn about shortly, play a similar role.

Judging credit risk is the business of credit-rating services, often called agencies even though they are companies. Standard & Poor's, Moody's Investors Service, and Fitch Ratings are the three largest services. They analyze governments, or sovereigns, and companies, and they assign ratings to their debt. Although the borrower usually pays for the ratings, there are exceptions for sovereign debt. When a government doesn't pay, the rating is said to be unsolicited.

Bill ratings start at A-1+ for S&P, P-1 for Moody's, and F1+ for Fitch. The companies use fewer tiers, or levels, than they do for notes and bonds, which we'll see later. Only borrowers with high ratings typically can raise funds in the money market.

Interest rate risk is another concern, as higher rates translate into lower prices for bills and other debt securities. If the one-year Treasury bill rate in the earlier example climbed to 0.2 percent the next day from 0.1 percent, the price would fall by about $10 for every $1,000 face amount. Investors who sell the security or have to reflect its value in their financial statements would suffer losses.

Lower rates, on the other hand, pose reinvestment risk. This refers to the inability to earn as much on a similar investment when payments are received. The risk is minimal in our example, because the one-year bill rate can't fall too far from 0.1 percent. If the rate was 1 percent, or perhaps 10 percent, then the risk would be far greater.

Inflation risk, or the threat that price increases will reduce the buying power of whatever money you receive, is present as well. This would turn into a reality in our 0.1 percent example as long as the Consumer Price Index (CPI), the most widely followed gauge of inflation, increases at a faster rate. If the pace accelerates, then the risk will rise as well.

Government bills have relatively little risk by comparison with other fixed-income securities. First, the government can raise taxes or print more money if needed to pay its debts. Other borrowers don't have those options. That's why bill rates are often called risk-free even if that isn't exactly the case.

Second, the bills mature in no more than a year. This means there isn't much time for interest rates or inflation to cut into the value of the final payment or the potential return from reinvesting the money.

Relative Value

Is that 0.1 percent bill in our example, or some other security like it, worth buying or something to avoid? We can make relative-value comparisons to help us answer the question.

Let's consider how the 0.1 percent rate stacks up against one-year Treasury bill rates over time. For the 10-year period that ended in 2008, the rate was about 4.5 percent on average. By that standard, the bills earn next to nothing. Then again, the bill rate fell below 1 percent from 2009 onward, which means the gap with 0.1 percent isn't so wide. Exhibit 2.6 shows the historical rates.

Then you can look at how the discount rate compares with similar rates for three- and six-month bills. Let's assume the three-month rate is 0.005 percent, and the six-month rate is 0.05 percent. This means

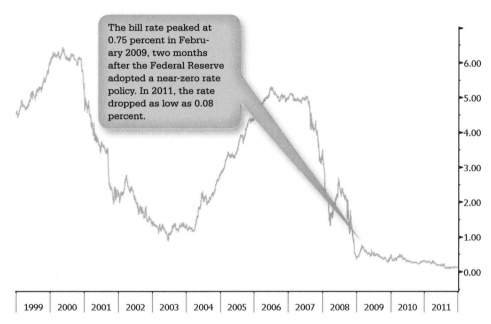

The bill rate peaked at 0.75 percent in February 2009, two months after the Federal Reserve adopted a near-zero rate policy. In 2011, the rate dropped as low as 0.08 percent.

Exhibit 2.6: One-Year Treasury Bill Rates
Source: U.S. Federal Reserve.

the one-year bill will return 20 times as much if you tie up your money for four times longer or twice the amount for investing twice as long. The comparisons may make the 0.1 percent rate look better.

Investors can plot each rate on a graph and connect the dots between them. The result is a rate curve, used to compare government bills with other types of securities. We'll revisit this topic when we run across another type of curve for notes and bonds.

Suppose you shunned the one-year Treasury bills and bought one-year securities sold by some other

government, or a company. The borrower might well be a bigger credit risk than the U.S. government. If that turns out to be the case, you ought to earn more for turning over your money.

How much more? The answer provides another way to judge relative value. Let's assume the other investment has a 0.5 percent discount rate. Subtract the 0.1 percent bill rate to calculate the gap between them: 0.4 percentage point. The figure is known as a rate spread and is expressed in basis points. So, you'll be able to earn another 40 basis points for your trouble.

DEFINITION:
Rate curve

Rate curves show borrowing costs over time by displaying discount rates as dots on a graph and then connecting the dots. Rate spreads are differences in rates between two securities, or two points on a curve.

To determine if 40 basis points is a little or a lot, you can look at whether the spread has widened or narrowed over time. You can determine how much more credit risk you would be taking with the other borrower, rather than the government.

Notes and Bonds

Considering how much money the United States borrows these days, could you possibly imagine that the country didn't sell bonds regularly during its first two centuries? Well, it's true if only technically.

There's a distinction made in the Treasury market and elsewhere between notes, which mature in two to 10 years, and bonds, which last for longer periods. The only U.S. securities that fit into the latter category are 30-year bonds.

Regular sales of 30-year Treasuries started in February 1977, more than two centuries after the Declaration of Independence was adopted. They were suspended in October 2001 because the country had budget surpluses and resumed in February 2006.

Along the way, the government raised money from bond investors through sales of notes as well as bills. These days, notes maturing in two, three, five, seven, and 10 years are sold on a set schedule.

The price the government pays to borrow in note and bond sales is called the yield. The yield is set by financial companies who buy the securities when they're first sold and by the investors who trade them afterward. It's based on the price of the notes and

bonds and the rate at which they pay interest. Lower yields translate into higher prices, and vice versa.

We'll take a closer look at yield shortly. For now, it's enough to know that Treasury yields are a benchmark, or point of reference, for the cost of borrowing. Yields for notes and bonds sold by U.S. agencies, other countries, and companies are tied to the yield on Treasuries that mature at about the same time. The gap in yields largely determines which securities investors want to buy, sell, or hold.

To understand why Treasury notes and bonds are benchmarks—and Treasury bills, too—let's review the reasons why the bills can be a safe investment. The federal government has the power to impose taxes, which other governments don't have to the same extent and companies don't have at all. The central bank has the ability to create money, which sets apart the government from every other borrower.

Auctions are the primary market for Treasury notes and bonds. It's been this way since the 1970s, when the government dropped an earlier practice of selling securities at fixed prices. The New York Fed handles auctions on behalf of the Treasury as it does for bill sales.

Yields at these auctions are like discount rates for bills since they represent the Treasury's cost of borrowing. The government has generally been able to raise funds more cheaply since the 1980s. Yields are still well above zero as the 10-year note shown in Exhibit 2.7 illustrates.

Treasury notes are sold monthly. Each auction of two-year, three-year, five-year, and seven-year notes

DEFINITION:
Yield

Yield is the projected annual return on a bond, based on the current price and future interest payments

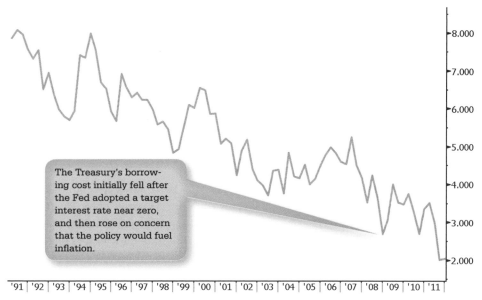

The Treasury's borrowing cost initially fell after the Fed adopted a target interest rate near zero, and then rose on concern that the policy would fuel inflation.

8.000
7.000
6.000
5.000
4.000
3.000
2.000

'91 '92 '93 '94 '95 '96 '97 '98 '99 '00 '01 '02 '03 '04 '05 '06 '07 '08 '09 '10 '11

Exhibit 2.7: Ten-Year Treasury Note's High Yield at Auction
Sources: U.S. Treasury, Bloomberg.

consists of new securities with their own maturity date. For 10-year notes, that's only true in February, May, August, and November. In other months, additional amounts of the most recent 10-year security are sold. These sales are called reopenings because they reopen an opportunity for investors to buy the notes. Thirty-year bond auctions work the same way as 10-year sales.

Regardless of the schedule or the maturity that's being sold, the government can count on offers from primary dealers. These firms make bids that specify a dollar amount and a yield, rather than the discount rate used for bills. The New York Fed accepts the lowest bids at which the sale can be completed.

Investors can buy notes and bonds from dealers or through the Treasury Direct program, as they can with bills. Other similarities exist between the auctions, based on details left out of the earlier discussion of bill sales.

Bids are competitive or noncompetitive, depending on whether there's a yield specified. Primary dealers may submit competitive bids on their own behalf and noncompetitive offers for clients. Treasury Direct bids are noncompetitive as successful bidders have to accept the average yield.

Bidders are direct or indirect. Primary dealers and Treasury Direct participants make their bids directly. Indirect bidders must go through primary dealers, and foreign central banks are in this category. Auction results show the percentage of bids made indirectly and the percentage of bonds sold to indirect bidders.

The bid-to-cover ratio, an indicator of demand, is made available for each auction. It's calculated by dividing the dollar value of bids by the dollar value of securities sold. If the ratio for a $10 billion note sale was 3.25, the ratio would mean investors sought to buy $32.5 billion of the securities. By comparing the 3.25 with previous ratios for similar note sales, you can assess how motivated the bidders were.

Once the notes and bonds are sold, they begin trading in the secondary market. Trades are made over the counter through the same electronic networks that handle the buying and selling of bills. Exchanges aren't part of the Treasury market though they play a role in other countries' debt markets.

Quotations

There's more than one type of quotation for Treasury notes and bonds, and it's worth looking at a couple of formats to find out what we'll see (see Exhibits 2.8 and 2.9).

The prices in the two quotes are about the same as they show the same Treasury note. The first one resembles the bill quote in Exhibit 2.5 except that the numbers differ. To find out why, let's go through the details.

T: Symbol for Treasury notes and bonds.

2 1/8: Annual interest rate, or **coupon rate, in percentage** points. The note's owner will receive 2 1/8 percent of face value, or $2.125 for every $1,000 invested, each year until maturity.

▲
▼   T 2 ⅛ 08/15/21   ↑ 103-20 +1-07 103-19+/103-20
    At 14:42 Op 102-13¾   Hi 103-28+ Lo 102-13 Prev 102-13 CBBT

Exhibit 2.8: A Treasury Note Quote, Part 1

▲
▼   US TREASURY N/B   T 2 ⅛ 08/15/21 103-19¾ /103-20¼ (1.73 /72) CBBT @14:41

Exhibit 2.9: A Treasury Note Quote, Part 2

08/15/21: Maturity date in month/day/year format.

Up arrow: The uptick/downtick arrow tracks prices this time around. When it's up, the last price change was an increase, and vice versa.

103-20: Price of the note as a percentage of face value. Here, it's 103 percent and then some. The 20 means 20/32 of a percentage point, as Treasury notes and bonds are quoted in fractions, and the standard denominator is 32. The price is 103 20/32 percent, which is the same as 103 5/8 percent.

+1-07: Change on the day in fractions of a point. The note rose 1 7/32, or about $1.22 for every $1,000 invested.

103-19+/103-20: Bid and ask prices for the note, in percentages of face value. The + sign that ends the bid price indicates that it's halfway between 103 19/32 and 103 20/32. (The second quote's bid price ends with 19 3/4 divided by 32, which means the full number is 103 79/128. The ask price ends with 20 1/4, making the number 103 81/128. Bond-market fractions get even smaller sometimes.)

At 14:42: Time of the quote, using the 24-hour clock.

Op 102-13 3/4, Hi 103-28+, Lo 102-13, Prev 102-13: Opening, high, and low prices for the current day, and the close from the previous day. The opening price is 102 55/128, as the fraction equals 13 3/4 divided by 32. The high is between 103 28/32 and 103 29/32, as the + indicates.

CBBT: Source of the price information. This is a composite quote from Bloomberg BondTrader, as the Treasury bill quote was earlier.

A pair of figures appears only in the second quote: 1.73/1.72. This shows the bond's yield at the bid and ask prices. Yield is based on the note's annual interest rate—in this case, 2 1/8 percent—and the difference between the market price and face value.

Why would the note yield less than 2 1/8 percent, as it does here? Go back and look at the 103–20 price. Any investor who pays that much will lose 3 5/8 percent of the security's face value at maturity. If the price was less than 100 instead, then the yield would exceed 2 1/8 percent.

Three Rs

Returns, the first of the three Rs, and yields are much the same for government notes and bonds. If investors buy a security and put it away until maturity, it's a safe bet the interest will be paid on time and the principal amount, or face value, will be paid off. Changes in yield won't affect returns unless they sell the security before the maturity date.

Even so, the risks confronting buy-and-hold investors rise over time. Inflation has more of an opportunity to cut into the value of note and bond payments. Interest rates have more room to fall, reducing the income from reinvesting those funds when they're received. There's more time for the government's finances to worsen, hurting its ability to borrow.

Relative-value comparisons are built around yields in the same way that the analysis of bills started with discount rates. It's possible to include bills in the analysis by calculating bond-equivalent yields, based on the assumption that they paid interest.

Returns

Our discussion of yield touched on the two main components of bond returns. The first is interest, which is paid according to a set schedule. The second is the purchase price relative to the face amount, or principal, repaid at the maturity date.

Not all government notes and bonds pay interest and principal the same way. Some account for inflation, which otherwise reduces the value of bond payment. Others have a single payment at maturity, like government bills. Let's find out how these differences affect returns.

Fixed-rate debt accounts for most of the Treasury's borrowing. The 10-year note is a perfect example. The annual interest rate and the face amount stay the same until maturity. In other words, they're fixed. Anyone who bought the note at the quoted price and kept the security until August 15, 2021, would be assured of a 1.73 percent annual yield at current market rates.

The 1.73 percent figure represents a nominal return, as it doesn't take inflation into account. The real return can only be estimated because it's ultimately based on price changes for the next 10 years. Consumer prices would have to increase about 1.75 percent a year to send the real return below zero. The higher the inflation rate, the more a bond investor suffers.

Inflation-indexed notes and bonds are designed to adjust for shifts in inflation rates. Treasury Inflation-Protected Securities, called TIPS, are the U.S. government's version. The principal amount changes along with the CPI, and the government pays the adjusted principal at maturity as long as the CPI has risen. Quotes on TIPS show the real yield rather than the nominal yield. If 10-year TIPS have a 0.48 percent yield, for instance, anyone buying and holding them can expect to earn 0.48 percent after inflation each year for the next decade, based on current market rates.

To gauge the outlook for inflation, subtract TIPS yields from those on fixed-rate Treasuries maturing about the same time. The 10-year note yield of 1.73 percent minus our 10-year TIPS yield, 0.48 percent, equals 1.25 percentage points. That's how much consumer prices may increase each year, on average, in the next decade. Exhibit 2.10 shows how the gap between fixed-rate yields and TIPS, an implied inflation rate, compares with changes in consumer prices over time.

TIPS are a variation on floating-rate bonds, where the interest payments vary or float along with a specified market interest rate. We'll have more on these later, as the Treasury doesn't sell floating-rate debt.

Zero-coupon securities aren't sold directly by the U.S. government either. Securities firms create them from fixed-rate and inflation-indexed notes and bonds. Each interest payment is transformed into a separate security as is the principal payment. The

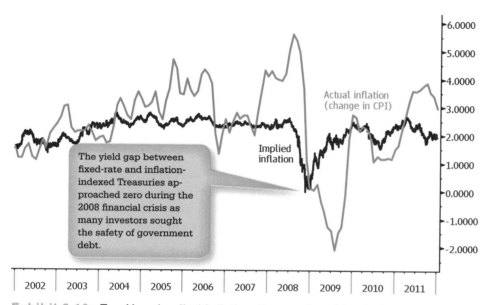

The yield gap between fixed-rate and inflation-indexed Treasuries approached zero during the 2008 financial crisis as many investors sought the safety of government debt.

Exhibit 2.10: Ten-Year Implied Inflation Rate and 12-Month Change in Consumer Price Index

result is Separate Trading of Registered Interest and Principal Securities (STRIP or STRIPS).

STRIPS are similar to government bills, except that most of them take longer than a year to mature. The buyer pays less than face value and receives the full amount at maturity in a single payment. The gap between market price and face value closes over time, which means an investor has to pay income taxes on STRIPS each year even though income isn't paid out.

Companies raise money by selling fixed-rate debt, along with other types of notes and bonds. We'll look at the possibilities in more detail later.

Risks

The risks of owning government notes and bonds increase over time. They depend on the amount of money you receive as an investor and the amount of time that passes until each payment arrives.

To illustrate, let's compare a 10-year Treasury note and a 10-year STRIP as investments. Assume that both securities have a face value of $1,000 and a coupon of 2 percent.

Owners of the note receive $10 every six months, as it pays interest twice a year, plus $1,000 at maturity. This means they get a total of $1,200. If they buy the security at an auction, they will only have to wait six months before the money starts rolling in.

The interest payments make the note less risky than the STRIP even though they mature at the same time. They amount to $200, or one-sixth of the $1,200 total, and all but the last one arrives before the 10 years are up. Investors in the STRIP receive $1,000, and all the money comes at maturity.

An indicator called duration shows the note is a safer bet. Duration is the time period investors will have to wait for the amount they initially invested to be returned. It's based on what all the payments are worth today, or their present value.

The note's duration is about nine years, thanks to the 2 percent annual interest rate. The STRIP has a 10-year duration, matching its maturity date.

Modified duration, a similar figure, shows how much the note's price would rise or decline if the yield changed by one percentage point. This figure is a percentage rather than a number of years. The modification has to do with how interest is calculated.

Now that you've seen how bond investors gauge risk, let's remind ourselves where it comes from. Credit risk, interest rate risk, inflation risk, and reinvestment risk affects government notes, and bonds, as well as bills.

S&P, Moody's, and Fitch, the largest rating services, are among those assessing credit risk. AAA ratings have become synonymous with the least risky borrowers, and we have S&P to thank for that. Moody's

has a different top rating, Aaa. Fitch uses AAA. Treasuries had these ratings across the board before 2011, when S&P cut the United States for the first time.

All three companies use the letters A, B, and C in their bond-rating systems. S&P's scale includes plus and minus signs as well. Moody's uses the small "a" along with the number 1, 2, or 3 for several ratings below Aaa. Fitch uses pluses and minuses in much the same way as S&P does, and both include a fourth letter in their scales, D, meaning default.

We'll revisit the credit ratings later when we look at corporate notes and bonds. For the moment, it's enough to know there's more time for them to worsen while notes and bonds are outstanding than there is with bills. The same holds true for investors' outlook, which may or may not be in line with the assessments made by rating companies.

Risk and time are linked for interest rates, inflation, and reinvestment as well. Let's take inflation as an example. If consumer prices increase 2 percent a year, the value of a $1,000 payment on a note or bond will be about $780 after 10 years. That's far below the $980 value after one year, the longest maturity date for a Treasury bill.

Relative Value

When investors consider whether a note or bond is cheap, expensive, or fairly priced, they inevitably look at yield. It's a common denominator for debt securities regardless of who sold them, which currency they are denominated in, when and how they pay interest, or any other detail.

There are yields at two, three, five, seven, and 10 years to consider for Treasury notes, along with yields on 30-year bonds. We can add one-month, three-month, six-month, and one-year bills to the mix by assuming they paid interest and by adjusting their discount rates accordingly.

Graphs come in handy to see how they compare as they did for bills. There's a dot for each security, whose position depends on the yield and the amount of time to maturity. The dots are joined into a yield curve, which shows how much it might cost to borrow for other periods (see Exhibit 2.11).

The line in this graph rises along with the time to maturity. This means the yield curve is upward sloping, which is usually the case. Investors get paid more for lending money to the government for longer.

Curves don't always look this way. When the central bank is raising interest rates to restrain inflation, yields may fall over time rather than rise. That can

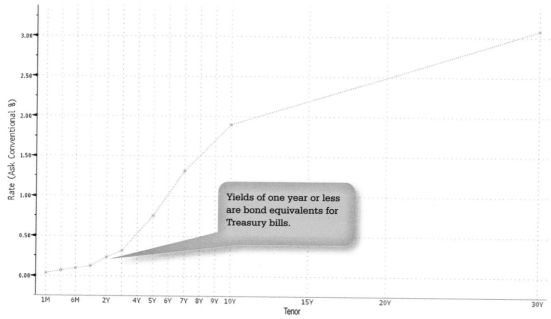

Exhibit 2.11: Treasury Yield Curve

happen because bill yields are more closely linked to Fed policy than note and bond yields, which are more influenced by the inflation outlook.

When curves slope downward, they are said to be inverted. This kind of shape has historically pointed toward slower economic growth at best, and a recession at worst, because it signals the central bank wants to discourage borrowing.

At other times, there's little difference in bill, note, and bond yields. The curve looks like a straight line, and it's said to be flat. Curves can flatten as they shift from being upward sloping to inverted, and vice versa.

Regardless of how the curve appears, differences in yield will occur among the depicted bills, notes, and bonds. This leads to another way of judging relative value: looking at those gaps, or yield spreads, the bond market's equivalent of rate spreads.

We can do this with securities on the curve. Ten-year Treasury notes yielded about 2 percent, while two-year notes yielded about 0.25 percent. In other words, bond investors stood to earn about 175 basis points by lending money to the government for eight more years. The differential was in line with historical standards as shown in Exhibit 2.12.

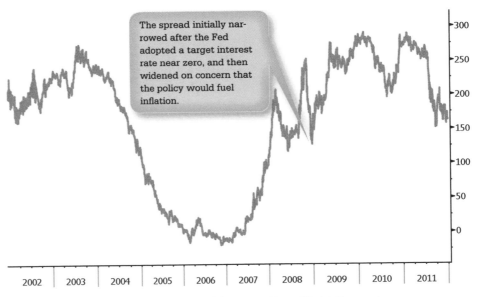

Exhibit 2.12: Two-Year/Ten-Year Treasury Note Yield Spread

The spread narrowed to about zero in February 2006 and turned negative for much of the following year, as the chart depicts. When two-year and 10-year yields are about the same, the yield curve flattens. When their spread is less than zero, the result is an inverted curve.

Similar comparisons can be made among Treasuries and other types of U.S. government debt, and between the United States and other countries. Investors do so regularly as they search for what's cheap, expensive, and fairly priced.

There's more to relative-value comparisons than yield curves and yield spreads as you might imagine. We'll see the effect of credit ratings, for example, when we look at corporate notes and bonds. For the moment, it's enough to know the central role that curves and spreads have to play.

Video:
Treasury yields, curves, and spreads

www.wiley.com/go/bvgfinancialmarkets

Test Yourself

Answer the following multiple-choice questions:

1. Currencies quoted in dollars per unit, rather than units per dollar, include:
   a. Euro.
   b. British pound.
   c. Australian dollar.
   d. All of the above.
   e. a and b only.

2. Governments affect the value of currencies through:
   a. Pegging.
   b. Intervention.
   c. Devaluation.
   d. All of the above.
   e. b and c only.

3. Treasury-bill returns come from:
   a. Price changes.
   b. Interest payments.
   c. Dividend payments.
   d. All of the above.
   e. a and b only.

4. Treasury note and bond returns come from:
   a. Price changes.
   b. Interest payments.
   c. Dividend payments.
   d. All of the above.
   e. a and b only.

5. The Treasury yield curve is usually:
   a. Flat.
   b. Inverted.
   c. Upward sloping.
   d. Humped.
   e. All of the above.

Answers: 1. d; 2. d; 3. a; 4. e; 5. c

CHAPTER 3

Companies

Companies have more ways to raise money than the government does. They can borrow by selling the equivalent of Treasury bills and by making other arrangements to borrow funds for a year or less. They can sell notes and bonds, occasionally or regularly. They can sell shares, which enables them to bring in new owners and allows current investors to increase their stakes.

Each of these investments can be riskier than handing over money to a government. Companies can't compel anyone to buy their products or services, as the government can. There isn't any printing press that can come to their aid during business slumps.

These investments have degrees of risk as well. Equity holders can't count on receiving payments from the company, as the owners of corporate notes and bonds usually can. Companies aren't required to pay dividends on their shares, and some of the most successful ones don't. Owners of the stock can only hope the value of their holdings will rise over time.

The ultimate risk is that a company will be unable to meet its financial obligations and go bankrupt. Investors in U.S. government debt don't have to worry about that prospect. Let's look at how one bankruptcy shut down the money market, where the shorter-term borrowing is done.

Money Markets

Companies turn to the money market to borrow money for days, weeks, or months, typically to finance day-to-day operations. Lehman Brothers Holdings Inc., which filed for bankruptcy in September 2008, was among the financial companies that tapped the market by selling securities.

Lehman's collapse caused the value of investments in the firm to plunge. The losses hurt many investors who had seen the money market securities as a safe bet. The casualties included the Reserve Primary Fund, which was the country's oldest money market mutual fund.

Many investors responded by refusing to buy similar securities, regardless of the company selling them. Their retreat left the money market unable to function and forced a number of companies that raised money there to turn to bank borrowings and bond sales, which are more costly and time consuming. The U.S. government had to provide hundreds of billions of dollars in financial support to money funds, among the biggest buyers of the debt.

Fortunately, instances like this are rare. Companies can use the money market to borrow from investors as well as each other. They can gain access to financing in many ways, and they're all worth a look.

Banks can borrow directly from other banks in the United States through the federal funds market. The money comes from funds that have to be held in reserve under federal regulations. When a bank's reserves are too low, it's able to borrow to meet the minimum standard. When a bank has excess reserves, it can earn money by lending them.

The rate on overnight loans of federal funds, or fed funds for short, is significant. The Federal Reserve (Fed) sets a target for this rate through monetary policy, designed to contain inflation and maximize employment. Though the market rate will fluctuate from day to day, the Fed ensures it stays near the target. To meet this goal, the central bank adds and removes money from the banking system as needed through open market operations.

International banks borrow from and lend to each other in several financial centers, especially London, where rates are set for one-month to 12-month loans of dollars and other currencies. The British Bankers' Association surveys these rates each day and compiles averages. Each average is known as a London Interbank Offered Rate (Libor). The cost of borrowing for financial and non-financial companies alike is often tied to Libor, as we'll see later. Libor is available for several currencies and maturities, and Exhibit 3.1 illustrates rates in dollars.

Certificates of deposit (CDs) are another way for banks to raise money-market funds. These aren't the kind of CDs you'll see advertised at your local bank branch. They have denominations of $100,000 or more, which explains why they're often described as jumbo CDs. Larger investors and companies buy them to earn some money on their excess cash.

Bankers' acceptances (BAs) are part of the money market mix as well. They are used in international trade to help ensure a future payment will be made on time. Banks create them when an importer with enough money in its accounts asks the institution to take responsibility for the payment. The importer sends the acceptance to its supplier, which has the

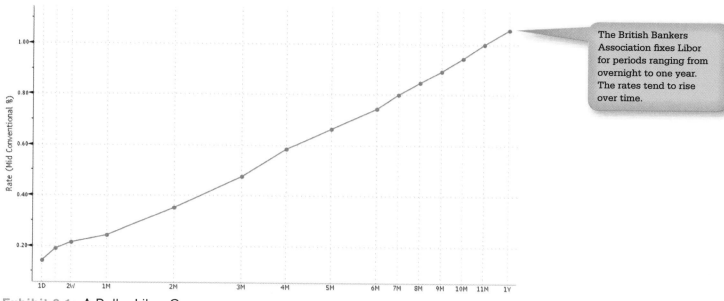

The British Bankers Association fixes Libor for periods ranging from overnight to one year. The rates tend to rise over time.

Exhibit 3.1: A Dollar Libor Curve

ability to raise cash right away by selling the agreement for less than face value.

Repurchase agreements (repos or RPs) enable securities firms as well as banks to finance investments. These agreements have two components, a sale of securities and a contract that requires the seller to buy them back later. The gap between the sale and repurchase prices provides a return to the buyer, who is effectively a lender. The buyer may seek higher returns by selling the borrowed security in a short sale.

Many of these agreements go through another bank or a clearinghouse, which ensures that both sides live up to their obligations. These are known as tri-party repos because there are three participants rather than two.

Repos are a type of secured financing, in which the securities serve as collateral. Many companies rely on unsecured financing, or borrowing that's based on a promise to pay. Investors lose if a company fails to keep the promise, as Lehman's lenders found out the hard way.

Even so, demand exists for securities that enable companies to borrow for as long as nine months without having to put up collateral. This type of debt is called commercial paper (CP), and it represents the corporate equivalent of Treasury bills.

Financial companies run CP programs to provide cash for daily operations. Automakers' finance units raise money this way as well because CP is a flexible way for these companies to borrow money.

Companies can file for U.S. regulatory approval to sell CP up to a specified dollar limit. Once they have clearance, they are free to choose which maturities to sell and when to sell them. Some companies sell securities daily, and others do so less often.

Not all CP is unsecured. Some banks and financial companies sell asset-backed paper through specially created units known as conduits. These units, also called special investment vehicles (SIVs), are set up to own assets that the company wants to get off its books. Many of them collapsed in the 2008 financial crisis because they owned mortgage-related securities. When the SIVs failed, the companies that started them had to take back the assets and suffered as a result.

The crisis took a toll on the CP market, especially because of Lehman's failure. Many investors shunned the market to avoid a similar disaster in the future. Many companies that sold the securities turned to bond sales so they wouldn't lose access to financing.

Combine fed funds, Libor, BAs, CDs, RPs, and CP, and you end up with a bowl of money market alphabet soup. You won't find this on a menu of investments for individuals. It's made for brokerage firms, banks, pension and endowment funds, money managers, and other institutional investors.

There's an emphasis on the primary market because it's easier to track than the secondary market for the securities. Companies that sell CP, for instance, regularly post discount rates for different maturities. After the securities are sold, finding their market rates may be difficult to do, if not impossible.

CP sellers can choose to adopt a do-it-yourself (DIY) approach or to have a securities firm do the work on their behalf. Securities that are sold without a middleman are labeled as direct issue, and those going through brokerages are dealer placed.

Quotations

Less detail is in quotes on companies' money market securities than there was earlier on Treasury bills. As an example, take a look at Exhibit 3.2, a quote on CP sold by General Electric's finance unit, GE Capital.

Rather than complain about what's missing, be thankful for what you have: a quote on an individual company

```
DIGEO90D ↑.14 unch
At 10:20  Op .14 Hi .14 Lo .14
```
Exhibit 3.2: A GE Capital Commercial-Paper Quote

that provides something more than the current discount rate. With that in mind, let's see what's here.

DIGE090D: DI stands for direct issue. GE Capital is among the companies that go directly to investors for funds, rather than having dealer-placed paper. GE designates the seller, General Electric Capital, GE's finance unit. The three numbers followed by a D stand for 90 days, the period from the initial sale to the maturity date. CP is sold for as long as 270 days, so the 0 before the 90 would be 1 or 2 in some cases.

Up arrow: The uptick/downtick arrow refers to the rate, as it did with Treasury bills, rather than price.

.14: Current rate of 0.14 percent, or 14 basis points.

unch: Rate change on the day. There wasn't one in this case.

At 10:20: Time of the quote, using the 24-hour clock. Companies usually make CP sales early in the day, as this quote suggests.

Op .14, Hi .14, Lo .14: Opening, high, and low rates for the current day. Here they show the rate was unchanged throughout the day.

Three Rs

Lehman's collapse showed that corporate money market investments can be riskier than government bills. At worst, investors may end up with unexpected losses on their holdings. Many investors are willing to take the additional risk anyway because of the potential for higher returns. They make relative-value comparisons similar to those we saw earlier for government securities. With that in mind, let's go through the three Rs.

Returns

Companies follow the government's example by avoiding interest payments on money market debt. Investors buy these securities at a discount to the face value, which they get at maturity. This means the difference between the purchase price and face amount counts the most in returns.

The discount is larger than it would be for a government security with the same terms. Otherwise, investors would lack a financial incentive for buying the corporate debt. CP sold directly by top-rated companies for three months might have a 0.2 percent discount rate, for example, when the comparable Treasury bill rate is near zero. That way, the securities will provide some income, unlike the government's debt.

The 0.2 percent figure may vary over time even if the government keeps paying next to nothing to borrow because the rate reflects supply and demand. Specifically, it's based on the value of securities being sold and the amount that investors are willing to put into them.

Risks

Now that we have moved to companies from governments, it's worth reviewing the risks that investors

> **KEY POINT:**
>
> The higher the discount rate, the riskier the investment. Rates on CP and other money market investments generally exceed those on government bills.

take in markets. The clearest is market risk, or the potential for prices to fall rather than rise. There's also liquidity risk, which is the inability to sell at the market price when raising cash.

CP and other money market investments are affected by these risks, along with those tied to the economy, politics, policy, and currency swings. Interest rate risk, inflation risk, and reinvestment risk are a concern though they're less of an issue than for notes and bonds because these securities mature in a short time.

Credit risk, on the other hand, takes on greater meaning. There's plenty of room for differences among companies as the rating scales from S&P, Moody's, and Fitch indicate. Investors have to take them into account in determining which securities are worth owning. The analysis is more complex than it is for Treasury bills, where they can focus on the U.S. government's ability to pay its debts.

Investors must deal with concerns that specifically affect corporate securities, starting with business risk, or the possibility that a company's performance will worsen. As the risk increases, so does the potential for a drop in cash flow, or the amount of money the company can use to cover debt payments and other expenses.

Event risk is a specific type of business risk, tied to an occurrence that may affect the company's ability to operate or to pay debts. Mergers and acquisitions can add to a company's debt burden and hinder its ability to compete. Splitting up a company or spinning off a business may mean less cash is available to meet obligations.

Industry risk can affect the value of companies and their securities as well. This is the threat that a company may suffer because of what's happening in its industry rather than its own actions. Consider what happened to photography, for example, when digital cameras replaced film cameras as the industry standard. The shift hurt Eastman Kodak Co. so badly that the company, once the world's largest maker of film, filed for bankruptcy. Fujifilm Holdings Inc. and other competitors also were affected.

Business risk, event risk, and industry risk are lower for corporate money market securities than for notes and bonds because of their shorter time to maturity. That said, the risks must be examined, as the Lehman example shows. They do much to explain the return gap between companies and governments.

Relative Value

Let's turn our attention to that 0.2 percent rate on CP. Considering that Treasury bill rates are close to zero, the two-tenths of a percentage point may be enough to draw some investors to the company's securities. Others might look at that additional return and conclude it isn't enough to compensate for the risk.

This is the kind of relative-value judgment that money market investors make daily. Others are similar to those cited with government bills, so let's run through the comparisons in summary form.

History: The 0.2 percent rate is tiny by historical standards. Top-rated U.S. companies paid three times as much to borrow in the CP market in mid-2010, according to data compiled by Bloomberg. In 2006 and 2007, the rate was more than 5 percent, or 25 times as high.

Different maturities: Companies sell CP for one to 270 days, so many other rates and time periods are available. Rate curves are more useful for this analysis than they are for Treasury debt, with four maturities sold regularly. Exhibit 3.3 shows how a curve might look for the highest-rated, directly placed CP.

Rate spreads may provide insight into what's cheap, expensive, or fairly valued as yield spreads did in the previous chapter. It's possible to compare spreads for any two maturities included on the curve.

Different credit ratings: CP is classified by rating. Borrowers rated A1+ by S&P and P1 by Moody's get the best deal. The rates they pay can be shown on a curve and compared with those of lower-rated companies.

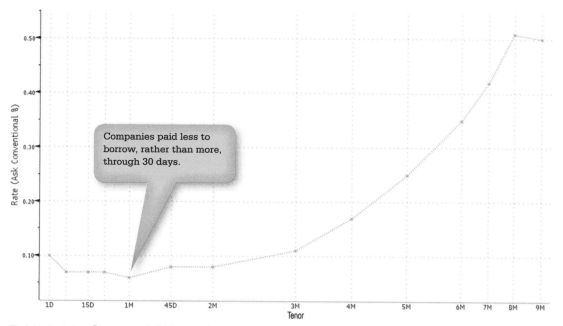

Exhibit 3.3: Commercial Paper A1+/P1 Direct Issue Rates

Direct issue vs. dealer placed: Companies that run their own CP sales pay lower rates on their borrowing than those who work with dealers. By tracking them separately, it's possible to compare their curves.

Different security types: Money market investors can buy asset-backed CP, rather than securities that carry only a promise to pay. They can dig into the alphabet soup we made earlier and come up with CDs or repos. These investments have rate curves, so it's possible to compare them with others or to look at specific rate spreads.

Notes and Bonds

Microsoft Corp. doesn't need to borrow money. The world's largest software maker once paid out $32.6 billion to investors because too much money was sitting around. Microsoft piled up billions of dollars more cash each year, thanks to the dominance of its Windows operating system and Office collection of word processing, spreadsheet, and presentation software for personal computers.

None of this stopped Microsoft from raising funds in the bond market. The first sale of debt, totaling $3.75 billion, was completed in May 2009. The company later borrowed billions of dollars more through additional sales.

Why would Microsoft go this route? Borrowing money didn't cost that much since the company received the highest possible credit ratings. Some of the funds were used to buy back stock, a way to reward shareholders. Some went to pay for an expansion of the company's business.

Companies without Microsoft's financial stability can raise money from bond investors for similar purposes. They may sell debt securities to help pay for takeovers, to refinance more costly borrowing, and to pay off earlier obligations, among other reasons.

Investors buy them, secured or unsecured, because they can provide higher returns than lending money to the government. To calculate how much higher, they compare yields on the securities with those on government notes or bonds that mature at about the same time. The difference between them is a yield spread, or premium, and shows what investors will earn for taking the added risk of lending to a company.

This risk can be small when a borrower's credit exceeds minimum ratings, defined as BBB– by S&P and Fitch and Baa3 by Moody's. Companies in the category are described as investment-grade borrowers, and the notes and bonds they sell are called investment-grade securities.

Ratings below the thresholds put companies into the high-yield category. They have to borrow in the non-investment-grade, or junk bond, market, which Michael Milken popularized at Drexel Burnham Lambert in the 1970s and 1980s.

Some investors avoid buying junk-rated debt on principle. Others are willing to invest as long as the

DEFINITION:
Investment-grade

Investment-grade bonds exceed rating thresholds set by S&P, Moody's, and Fitch. High-yield, or junk, bonds are below them.

potential returns are high enough. Either way, high-yield notes and bonds are prone to bigger gains and losses than investment-grade issues. Exhibit 3.4, a chart of yield indexes compiled by the Financial Industry Regulatory Authority (FINRA), an independent regulator, and Bloomberg, shows the volatility.

As you can see, high-yield securities can be more lucrative than their investment-grade counterparts as long as the borrower makes payments on time. That's a bigger if, as we'll find out later.

Financial companies are among the biggest sellers of notes and bonds because their business is all about money. They raise funds to make loans and investments, and they profit by earning more than enough to cover their financing costs. Industrial, media and telephone companies and utilities also turn to bond investors regularly. They spend relatively large amounts of money on plants and equipment, and their businesses produce the kind of cash needed to make debt payments.

Some companies that borrow regularly to finance daily operations sell medium-term notes (MTNs). These securities are created and sold in much the same way as CP even though MTNs usually mature in one to 10 years and can last as long as 30 years.

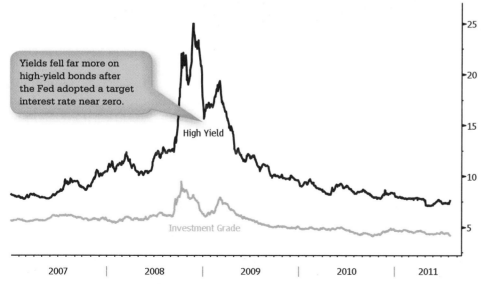

Yields fell far more on high-yield bonds after the Fed adopted a target interest rate near zero.

High Yield

Investment Grade

Exhibit 3.4: FINRA-Bloomberg Corporate Bond Yield Indexes

Most corporate notes and bonds are debentures, or unsecured loans. This means investors only have a company's promise to pay interest and repay the principal, or borrowed money, on time. If the promise isn't kept, they can't come and repossess any of its assets, as a bank can when people fail to keep up with mortgage and car payments.

Owners of secured corporate debt, on the other hand, are in the same position as the bank. The notes and bonds are backed by buildings, equipment, property, and other collateral. As an example, transportation companies sell securities backed by airplanes and railcars.

Many corporate notes and bonds are bought when they first go on sale and rarely, if ever, are traded later. This means bond investors pay considerable attention to what they can buy in the primary market.

Some companies raising money in the United States register each bond sale individually with regulators. Registrations can cover more than one type of security. For example, a company looking to sell five-year and 10-year notes and 30-year bonds at the same time can file one statement for all of them.

Once the documents are approved, one or more securities firms conduct the sale on the company's behalf. These firms, called underwriters, line up investors to buy the bonds and arrange for other banks and brokers to do the same.

Others use a different approach, especially for MTNs. These companies lay the groundwork for future sales by filing a document called a shelf registration.

They can then sell securities on a daily basis, as they would with CP, to provide funds as needed. They can also sell notes and bonds more quickly later on, which allows them to take advantage of favorable market moves.

Either way, yields and yield spreads provide a basis for setting prices and interest payments. Let's assume that XYZ Co. wants to sell 10-year notes and investors demand a yield spread of 205 basis points to buy them. One basis point equals 0.01 percentage point. So, if the 10-year Treasury note's yield is 2 percent, the XYZ yield will have to be 4.05 percent.

The bond's annual interest rate, or coupon, and price would be adjusted to produce the required yield. The coupon might be set at 4 percent a year for the sake of rounding. To lift the yield to 4.05 percent, the buyer would pay a bit less than face value.

Once corporate notes and bonds are sold, they trade in a secondary market that's primarily over the counter. Though it's possible to buy and sell some securities on the New York Stock Exchange (NYSE) or the Nasdaq Stock Market (NASDAQ), the amount of debt changing hands there is small.

Price information is easier to obtain for corporate debt than for government bonds because of the Trade Reporting and Compliance Engine (TRACE). TRACE was introduced in 2002 to collect secondary market trading data from securities firms, compile the figures, and send out the results. These days, it's run by FINRA, which oversees the firms and ensures they provide the required information.

Many corporate debt securities aren't displayed on TRACE. Finding prices for the notes and bonds can be difficult at best because they rarely trade. Bloomberg provides price estimates based on yields for similar securities, and we'll see one further on.

Quotations

There's quite a disparity in the amount of detail that bond quotes provide, as you may have guessed by now. The two-for-one display in Exhibits 3.5 and 3.6 provides an illustration.

For starters, these quotes are for two separate bonds. Their main similarity is they were sold by units of General Electric. The first quote is for a note from GE's finance unit, GE Capital, which started out as a 10-year security. The statistics include the first figure we have seen so far for volume, or the amount of trading. It's here because of TRACE, which provides real-time prices for a fee and delayed prices free.

The second is for a bond sold by a GE unit, Security Capital Group, which originally matured in 30 years. The price is an estimate made by Bloomberg, using the yield on comparable securities as a guide.

Let's go through these quotes and find out what they have to offer. We'll focus on the first and mention the second along the way.

GE: Symbol for General Electric, which begins the first quote and follows Security Capital's name in the second.

4 5/8: Annual interest rate of 4 5/8 percent, or 4.625 percent. The comparable rate for the bond is 7.7 percent. Rates can be stated as fractions or decimals, as these two examples suggest.

01/21: Month and year of maturity for the GE Capital note. The Security Capital quote has an exact date, 06/15/28, in the month/day/year format.

$: Dollar-denominated security. GE sells bonds in several currencies, so the dollar sign is more than a formality.

```
GE 4 ⅝ 01/21 $ ↑ 104.310  +.101
At 13:19  Vol 50,797  Op 103.957  Hi 105.980  Lo 103.887  YLD 4.062  TRAC
```

Exhibit 3.5: A GE Capital Bond Quote

```
SECURITY CAP GRP GE 7.7 06/15/28   144.0237/144.0237   (4.04/4.04) BFV  @16:55
```

Exhibit 3.6: A GE Unit's Bond Quote

Up arrow: The uptick/downtick arrow, tied to price changes this time.

104.310: Price of the note as a percentage of face value. It's in decimals rather than the fractions used for Treasuries. A buyer would have to pay $1,043.10 for every $1,000 face amount. The price for the Security Capital bond would be $1,440.237, as it's valued at 144.0237 percent of the face amount.

+.101: Change from the previous day's close in percent.

At 13:19: Time of the quote, using the 24-hour clock.

Vol 50,797: Number of notes traded today. Each note has a face value of $1,000, which means about $50.8 million of the securities were traded. Other quotes show a dollar amount in place of this kind of number.

Op 103.957, Hi 105.980, Lo 103.887: Opening, high, and low prices for the current day.

Yld 4.062: Yield, rounded to three decimal places, at the current price.

TRAC: TRACE, the source of the GE note's price. The Security Capital bond was priced using Bloomberg Fair Value (BFV), which compares the bond with similar securities and estimates the yield, then the price. This kind of estimate often has to be made because many securities are bought and held, rather than traded.

There's another piece of data that might have appeared in the quote for GE's note: **233 bp vs T2.625 11/15/20.** It's the difference in yield between the security and a 10-year Treasury maturing at about the same time.

The bp stands for basis points, which means the GE yield is 233 basis points higher than the Treasury note yield. The spread is the additional amount you're paid as an investor to take the risk of lending money to the company, which can't impose taxes or print money as the government can.

The gap is equivalent to 2.33 percentage points. Subtract that amount from the 4.06 percent yield on GE's security after rounding, and you'll be left with the Treasury note's yield at the time: 1.73 percent, in line with what we saw earlier. The yield differential usually fluctuates over time, as Exhibit 3.7 illustrates.

Three Rs

When we looked at government notes and bonds, we started with the idea that yields and returns are similar. This may not be true for corporate debt, as these securities are designed to give companies more flexibility in managing their finances.

Interest payments on many corporate securities are linked to a market interest rate. This means they will fluctuate from one period to the next rather than staying the same. Investors can't be sure how much interest they will receive while owning the debt.

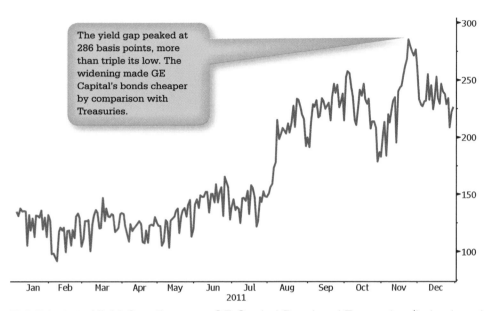

The yield gap peaked at 286 basis points, more than triple its low. The widening made GE Capital's bonds cheaper by comparison with Treasuries.

Exhibit 3.7: Yield Gap Between GE Capital Bond and Treasuries (in basis points)

In some cases, investors don't know how long they will be able to own the debt either. The issue arises because companies sell notes and bonds they can buy back before the maturity date at a set price. This feature allows them to take advantage of future declines in interest rates by refinancing at a lower cost.

These kinds of bells and whistles have to be built into return calculations and relative-value comparisons, which makes them more difficult. They heighten some risks we have seen before and introduce others we haven't. Let's look at the three Rs with those points in mind.

Returns

Investors make money on corporate notes and bonds in two ways as they do with government debt. They are assured of receiving interest payments, based on a schedule that's set when the securities are first sold. They stand to benefit from any market-price increases though the debt will be repaid at face value when the maturity date rolls around.

Fixed-rate corporate debt pays the same amount of interest every time. The market price of the note or bond fluctuates to keep the yield in line with current interest rates. When rates rise, companies benefit

STEP-BY-STEP:
FLOATING-RATE
INTEREST

1. ABC Inc. sells 10-year floating-rate notes. They pay interest twice a year at three-month dollar Libor plus 75 basis points.
2. Six months after the sale, Libor is 0.5 percent. Add the spread, and the note's annual interest rate is 1.25 percent.
3. ABC's first payment is half the annual rate. That's 0.625 percent, or 62.5 cents for every $1,000 borrowed.
4. One year after the sale, Libor is 0.75 percent. The annual rate rises to 1.5 percent.
5. ABC's second payment is 0.75 percent, or 75 cents per $1,000.

from having lower-cost financing. When they decline, investors profit because the future interest payments become more valuable.

Companies also sell floating-rate notes and bonds, where only the timing of interest payments is preset. The amount that's paid each time depends on a market rate such as Libor, which we discussed earlier. Payments are usually based on a spread to Libor for a specified currency and maturity date, often three months.

Floating-rate debt makes sense for companies whose income rises and falls along with interest rates. Banks are among them because they provide credit cards, make commercial loans, and buy securities whose interest payments float. Companies looking for rates to fall may favor floating-rate notes and bonds, which assure them of lower interest expense as long as their outlook is accurate.

Some companies sell inflation-indexed securities, similar to the U.S. government's Treasury Inflation-Protected Securities (TIPS). Changes in an inflation gauge such as the Consumer Price Index (CPI) replace Libor, or some other market rate, in the formula for calculating interest.

Returns on corporate notes and bonds depend on whether they remain outstanding until maturity. Some of these securities are callable, which means companies are allowed to buy them back in advance. A 30-year bond that can be called after five years would effectively turn into a five-year note if the company repurchases the debt.

Callable securities have what's called a yield to worst, which assumes they are bought back at the first possible opportunity. This yield can be calculated because call prices are set when the notes and bonds are first sold.

Corporate debt can be putable. Investors owning these securities would be able to sell them back to the company at predetermined prices before they mature. This feature sets a floor under the price of the notes and bonds, which aids returns. Call provisions have the opposite effect, as they give companies the right to buy their debt at what may be below-market prices.

Companies can sell convertible notes and bonds, which can be exchanged for common stock at a set price for each share. The ability to convert may belong to the investor, the company, or both, depending on the terms of the security. We'll revisit convertibles later, when we look more closely at variations on investing in companies.

Risks

We have seen three levels of risk that investors take in buying corporate notes and bonds. The first is the broadest, consisting of market risk, liquidity risk, economic risk, political risk, policy risk, and currency risk. The second combines credit risk, interest rate risk, inflation risk, and reinvestment risk, which are concerns for anyone owning debt securities. Real returns, adjusted for inflation, take this level of risk into account.

Business risk, event risk, and industry risk amount to a third level, focused on companies. A more specific business risk for note and bond investors is worth adding: bankruptcy risk, which Lehman's investors learned about the hard way. If a company's performance suffers enough, it may be unable to stay in business without seeking court protection from creditors. The reorganization that follows often results in losses for note and bond investors, among others.

While we're at it, we might add a bankruptcy-related threat to the second level: default risk. It's the most extreme form of credit risk. Companies default when they don't pay interest or repay principal on their debt as required. This can take place because they don't have the money or because they decide to keep their cash instead. Bankruptcy risk and default risk increase with the amount of time until corporate debt matures. That's why they're especially relevant here. We could have mentioned them in the discussion of money market securities, based on the Lehman example.

Call risk deserves a mention because of the earlier reference to callable notes and bonds. When interest rates fall, companies have more of an incentive to refinance or repay the debt to reduce interest expense. This would cause bond investors to lose years of interest payments at above-market rates. They would get back their original investment sooner than they wanted and would have to settle for lower returns if the funds were reinvested in similar securities.

Relative Value

Yield, especially in the form of curves and spreads, is a guidepost for determining whether corporate notes and bonds are cheap, expensive, or fairly valued. The same kinds of analysis we learned about earlier for government debt can be done with company securities. Let's run through them in summary form.

History: The easiest way to judge whether a yield is low, high, or somewhere in between is to look at where it's been. This usually has to be done on a security-specific basis because most companies don't sell securities with the consistency of the U.S. government. This means benchmark maturities are unavailable for comparisons.

Similar companies: Yield curves are available for categories of corporate notes and bonds that provide a benchmark for specific securities. If a bank note yields 4 percent and matures in five years, for example, the five-year yield on a curve of bank debt would shed light on the note's relative value.

Corporate curves are created differently than the Treasury curve. The connect-the-dots approach cited earlier won't work because there are too many maturities and yields to consider, including some for cheap or expensive securities.

Instead, the first step in creating a corporate curve is defining a debt category. Industry groups and credit ratings are among the criteria. Financial, industrial, media and telephone companies, and utilities can have their own curves. There may be one curve for companies with top ratings from S&P and Moody's, another for ratings one level lower, and so on.

Once the category is created, a group of corporate notes and bonds is compiled. Their yields and maturity dates are run through a mathematical formula to calculate the curve, which comes closest to fitting them all.

Different industries: Financial companies can be broken down into banks, broker-dealers, insurance companies, and real estate owners. Relative-value comparisons among these segments are made possible through industry-specific yield curves. It's possible, for instance, to track the spread between five-year notes on banks and insurers and decide which offers more value.

Different credit ratings: This kind of analysis can focus on yields for investment-grade and high-yield securities as a group. Spreads between the two categories enable investors to determine how much more they would earn by putting money into companies rated below BBB- at S&P and Baa3 at Moody's.

Investors can compare yields for similar corporate borrowers at different rating levels. S&P and Moody's ratings provide a basis to create rating-specific curves for banks, industrial companies, and others.

Different borrowers: Corporate yield curves are directly comparable to those on government debt even though they are compiled differently. The Treasury curve is a benchmark for gauging the relative value of companies' notes and bonds.

There's a comparison between top-rated industrial debt and Treasuries in the following chart. As you might expect, yields on the corporate securities are higher (see Exhibit 3.8).

Similar comparisons are possible between companies and other government-related borrowers that we have yet to cover. We'll touch on those later. Now it's time to shift our focus toward equity, as in stock, and away from debt.

Stocks

"How's the market doing?" The question could refer to any of the financial markets we have examined or any of the ones we'll consider in later chapters, but it doesn't. You could insert "stock" before "market" by default.

This is true because individuals and institutional investors have bought and sold shares in the United States for more than two centuries. Stocks tend to account for a bigger percentage of their holdings than any other asset. Share prices tend to fluctuate more than bond prices and money market rates each day.

All the interest in stocks works to the benefit of companies looking to raise money. They can sell shares and obtain funds they don't have to repay. It's good for corporate executives, financial backers, and others with stakes in a company because it gives them the opportunity to turn their holdings into cash.

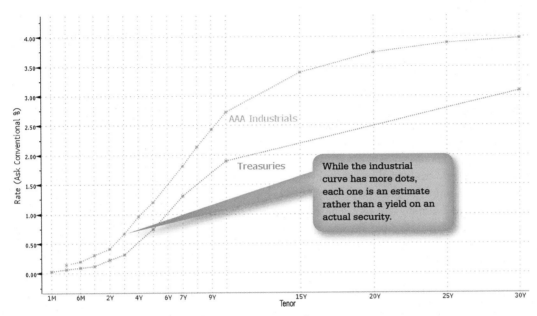

While the industrial curve has more dots, each one is an estimate rather than a yield on an actual security.

Exhibit 3.8: AAA Industrial and Treasury Yield Curves

The fewer shares there are, the greater the percentage of ownership that each share provides, and vice versa. If a company had 1,000 shares outstanding, for instance, then each share would amount to a 0.1 percent stake. If there are a million instead, then a share is only 0.0001 percent of the total.

Any other benefits of owning shares are up to the company that sells them. Voting rights and dividend payments are two of the most widely available perks.

Stockholders select the members of a company's board of directors, approve the outside accounting firm that audits its financial statements, accept or reject takeover bids, and decide other issues. Some companies ensure a smaller number of holders make these decisions by creating non-voting and voting shares. Others accomplish the same goal by having a separate class of stock with extra votes for each share.

Dividends are taken out of a company's profits, and the payments are usually made quarterly. Companies can go without them if they need the funds to finance expansion or sustain their business. Those that make

STEP-BY-STEP: OWNERSHIP STAKES

1. Apple Inc. had 929.4 million shares outstanding in October 2011 when co-founder Steve Jobs died.
2. Jobs owned about 5.6 million shares at the time of his death.
3. Divide 5.6 into 929.4. The result shows Jobs left behind a 0.6 percent stake.

the distributions set a payout ratio, or a percentage of earnings, they want to maintain each year.

Companies can return cash to holders by buying back stock as well as paying dividends. The repurchases increase earnings per share by reducing the amount of outstanding stock. Let's suppose the company with 1 million shares posted a $1 million profit. The earnings would amount to $1 a share. If the company bought back 100,000 shares and reported the earnings, the $1 million would be divided among only 900,000 shares. That works out to $1.11 a share.

There's no obligation for companies to repurchase stock. They can do the opposite. Sales of stock and related securities, takeovers of other companies, and grants to executives are among the moves that increase the number of outstanding shares.

These kinds of actions can dilute earnings, or spread them over a greater number of shares. That $1 million profit would be 91 cents a share, for instance, if the company had 1.1 million shares outstanding. Increase the share count to 2 million, and the profit drops to 50 cents a share.

The number of shares outstanding often rises because a company sells new stock as mentioned earlier. These sales are done in the primary market, where companies make initial public offerings (IPOs) and sell additional shares.

IPOs result from a company's decision to become publicly traded. The company selects one or more securities firms to be underwriters. These firms work with the company to determine the sale's timing, the number of shares to be sold, and the price to charge for them. Underwriters line up other firms to take part in the share sale and investors to buy the stock.

Investors and executives can sell shares when a company goes public. This portion of the sale is a secondary offering even though it's occurring in the primary market. The difference is that the proceeds will go to whoever sells the shares, rather than the company. In some cases, secondary offerings account for an entire IPO.

Going public lays the foundation for companies to sell additional shares and raise more money. While these sales are sometimes called secondary offerings, the phrase doesn't apply when they involve new stock.

Newly public companies can be more rewarding than older ones. This was the case during the 2000s, when a Bloomberg index of U.S. companies in their first year of trading rose as the Standard & Poor's 500 Index fell. Exhibit 3.9 compares the indexes.

IPOs bring companies into the secondary market, where their stock trades daily. U.S. companies usually list their shares on the NYSE or the NASDAQ. The NYSE's roots go back to 1792 when brokers gathered under a buttonwood tree in New York to set rules for stock and bond trading. NASDAQ, an electronic market, followed in 1971.

The NYSE and NASDAQ compete for stock trading with BATS Global Markets Inc. and Direct Edge Holdings LLC, which own exchanges. All four companies operate multiple markets, which are linked electronically to help investors make the best possible

KEY POINT:

Secondary offerings are sales of existing stock even though the phrase is often used to describe sales of new shares after an IPO.

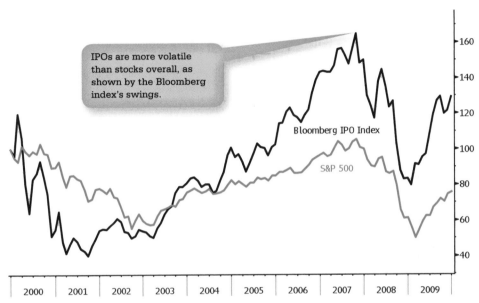

IPOs are more volatile than stocks overall, as shown by the Bloomberg index's swings.

Bloomberg IPO Index

S&P 500

Exhibit 3.9: Initial Public Offerings versus Standard & Poor's 500 Index (December 31, 1999 = 100)

deal on their trades. The NYSE is the only one with floor trading, where brokers buy and sell on an exchange floor.

The development of all-electronic markets has led to high-frequency trading, in which firms use computer-based buying and selling to profit from instantaneous market moves. The firms may own stock for a few seconds. Estimates of their share of trading in U.S. markets have been as high as 70 percent. Institutional investors can bypass exchanges and trade through dark pools, run by securities firms and others, where large blocks of stock change hands. The pools get their name because participants and public investors are kept in the dark about who's buying and selling and how many shares they have to trade.

Quotations

Stock quotes provide a level of detail we haven't run across before. Exchanges collect, consolidate, and distribute all kinds of trading data, including details about purchases and sales taking place on other markets. Let's check a quote for Apple Inc., which became the world's biggest company by market value in 2011, to see this for ourselves (see Exhibit 3.10).

AAPL: Apple's ticker, or stock symbol. U.S. tickers are no more than five letters. Use of one- to three-letter tickers was restricted to companies listed on the NYSE or the American Stock Exchange (AMEX) and four-letter tickers were reserved for listings on NASDAQ until 2007.

Companies can use one to four letters regardless of where they're listed, including the AMEX, now NYSE Amex. NASDAQ stocks with traditional tickers can have a fifth letter, which designates the type of security, a company in bankruptcy, or other conditions.

US: U.S. composite trading. Individual markets each have their own two-letter code on the Bloomberg terminal. The first letter is always U, designating a U.S. market. The second can appear alone in quotes.

$: Dollar-denominated security.

Up arrow: Uptick/downtick arrow, displaying the latest change in the stock price.

369.80: Price of the latest trade. U.S. share prices have been quoted in dollars and cents since 2001. Before then, they were quoted in fractions, just like Treasury notes and bonds.

−7.57: Change from the previous close. At the time of the quote, Apple was $7.57 lower on the day.

D: Second letter of the code for the Alternative Display Facility, where the latest price was posted. FINRA runs the facility to report on stock trades made outside NASDAQ.

P: Second letter of the exchange code for NYSE Arca, an electronic market owned by NYSE Euronext, where the bid price was posted. The letter originally stood for the Pacific Stock Exchange, a regional market with historical ties to NYSE Arca.

Down arrow: Uptick/downtick arrow, referring this time to the latest change in Apple's bid price.

369.60: Highest price that any potential buyer is willing to pay for Apple's shares.

/: Separator for the bid and ask price.

369.80: Lowest price that any potential seller will accept for Apple's shares.

Q: Second letter of UQ, the two-letter code for NASDAQ.

1 × 38: Number of round lots associated with the bid and ask prices. When combined with the earlier details, here's what the quote says: Someone wants

▲
▼ **AAPL** US $ ↑ **369.80** -7.57 D P↓369.60/369.80Q 1x38
At 16:30 Vol 19,108,791 Op 375.78 P Hi 377.74 D Lo 368.489 D

Exhibit 3.10: An Apple Inc. Stock Quote

to buy 100 shares of Apple at $369.60 each on NYSE Arca. Someone else is looking to sell 3,800 shares at $369.80 apiece on NASDAQ. This is known as the inside market, because the bid and ask prices are inside the range set by prices available in other markets.

At 16:30: Time of the latest price. In this case, it's the official close for the stock. Prices between 09:30 and 16:00, or 9:30 a.m. and 4 p.m. Eastern, are from the trading day.

Vol 19,108.791: Volume, or the number of shares changing hands during the current day. The total consists of round lots, or trades in multiples of 100 shares, and odd lots, or trades of fewer than 100 shares. Round lots are the standard for U.S. stocks.

Op 375.78 P, Hi 377.74 D, Lo 368.489 D: Opening, high, and low prices for the current day, along with the markets on which they were recorded. On this day, Apple opened at $375.78 on NYSE Arca. The high of $377.74 and the low of $368.489 both appeared on FINRA's facility. Note that the low price goes out to three decimal places, rather than two.

Quotes posted during the trading day would end the second line with a number like this: **ValTrd 4780.216m**. It's the dollar value of shares traded. The m is for $1 million, so the figure shows $4.78 billion of Apple shares changed hands.

Three Rs

Stocks are similar to corporate notes and bonds when it comes to returns and risks, the first two Rs that we'll consider. Dividends, like interest payments, are included in return calculations. Most of the risks that go with owning a company's shares affect its debt's value.

Relative value is where they part company. Though yields can show whether shares are cheap, expensive, and fairly priced, they aren't as encompassing a gauge as they are for bonds. For instance, yields based on dividends aren't meaningful for companies that don't pay them.

Earnings carry more weight with stock investors than bond investors, who are more concerned with a company's ability to pay debts. One of the most widely used relative-value gauges for stocks is the price-earnings ratio (P/E). It's calculated by dividing the stock's price by earnings per share, which can be historical or estimated.

Before we go any further, let's go through the three Rs in sequence to ensure we don't miss anything.

Returns

Dividends contribute to returns on stocks in the same way that interest affects bond returns, as mentioned earlier. The biggest difference is that there isn't any time limit on how long investors can

DEFINITION:
Price-earnings ratio

The price-earnings ratio (P/E) is the share price divided by earnings per share. The calculation is based on past or projected profits.

receive payouts because stocks don't have a maturity date.

The role that dividends play in returns increases with the amount of time an investor owns shares. Payouts accounted for 90 percent of U.S. stock returns between 1871 and 2009, according to a study done by Grantham, Mayo, Van Otterloo & Co. (GMO), a money management firm. The figure reflected dividend yields as well as inflation-adjusted growth in payouts, which James Montier, a member of GMO's asset allocation team, noted in an August 2010 report.

Investors don't make a habit of studying stock returns for 138-year intervals. They're more likely to focus on the latest quarter, the latest year, and some other relatively short period. Price changes affect returns far more than dividends for these periods.

When stocks don't pay dividends, investors can only make money if the price rises. Dividend-paying stocks, by contrast, can have positive returns even when the price drops. That's possible as long as the loss is smaller than the payout.

Dividends provide a financial cushion against losses. They enable investors to earn additional income by reinvesting the payouts. Shareholders in companies that keep their cash have to go without those benefits.

Risks

Shareholders can be perched at either end of the three levels of risk cited earlier. The first level consists of market risk, liquidity risk, economic risk, political risk, policy risk, and currency risk. The third touches on business risk, event risk, and industry risk along with the threat of bankruptcy.

Currency risk can be linked to a company's business rather than its shares. Many companies based outside the U.S. have American Depositary Receipts (ADRs), representing some number of shares. ADRs trade on the NYSE, NASDAQ, and other markets. They are also known as American Depositary Shares (ADSs).

Though ADRs are dollar-denominated, their owners still have to deal with currency risk. If the company is based in a country whose currency is losing value, then its shares are likely to fall as many international investors move their money elsewhere. The U.S.-listed securities will decline as well.

Currency risk can cut the other way because of its effect on a company's business. If the local currency rises in value, international sales and earnings may count for less when they're translated into that currency. The increase might lead to slower growth in revenue and profit, or even declines, as the company's products become more costly.

Bankruptcy risk is worth highlighting because it's more acute for shareholders than for any other investors in a company. When a company reorganizes, the holders have to settle for what remains after payments to banks, bondholders, and suppliers. In many cases, the shares are canceled, leaving the holders with nothing to show for their investment.

The second level of risk hasn't been mentioned because it's less of an issue for equity investors. Credit risk and default risk don't affect the value of securities directly. Inflation may be more of an opportunity than a risk as price increases can lead to higher sales, earnings, and share values. Interest rate risk and reinvestment risk are less of a concern because an investor can put dividend payments back into the stock, as opposed to settling for a lower-yielding investment.

Relative Value

Price has taken a back seat in our searches for relative value. That's no accident. Prices of government bills and other money market securities are an afterthought, designed to produce a specified discount rate. Note and bond prices are tied to the securities' face value, which the borrowers are obligated to pay at maturity. Little room exists for them to move without a substantial change in market interest rates.

Stock prices don't have these kinds of constraints. Though shares can have a face amount, known as a par value, they don't have to. When they do, it's often a fraction of a cent. That's fine for accounting purposes because par value isn't a sum of money that investors will receive in a few months or years.

Instead, the company's share price is driven by what's happening to sales, earnings, and dividend payments over time. Faster growth usually brings bigger gains for the stock, and declines can send the price lower.

The P/E ratio is one way to value stocks. Investors may use historical or projected earnings in their analysis, and each approach has merit. Historical earnings have the advantage of being more definite than estimates, which may not prove to be accurate. Then again, anyone buying a stock has to rely on future profits to push the share price higher. The past is useful as a guide to the future.

For the fastest-growing companies, historical P/Es will be higher than those based on projected earnings. For those growing more slowly, there may be little difference between the ratios.

Finding cheap, expensive, and fairly priced stocks may involve price-to-sales and price-to-cash flow ratios, calculated by dividing share prices by sales or cash flow per share rather than earnings. Another yardstick is book value, or the value of what a business owns minus what it owes. More precisely, book value shows what the company's assets are worth after subtracting liabilities.

We need to give yields their due as well, starting with dividend yields. They can be historical or estimated, like the earnings figures in P/E ratios. If the company with the $30 stock paid $1 a share in the past 12 months, then the shares have a dividend yield of 3.3 percent, or 1 divided by 30. If the company raised its payout rate to $1.20 a share, the projected dividend yield would be 4 percent.

There's a yield for earnings as well as dividends, which is useful for studying stocks without payouts. The earnings yield is the inverse of the P/E, or

**STEP-BY-STEP:
PRICE-EARNINGS RATIO**

1. ABC Inc.'s shares trade at $30.
2. ABC's earnings in the previous four quarters equaled $3 a share.
3. Divide the profit into the stock price for the P/E ratio, which is 10.

**STEP-BY-STEP:
ESTIMATED P/E RATIO**

1. ABC Inc.'s shares trade at $30.
2. Analysts expect next year's earnings to be $3.33 a share on average.
3. Divide the projection into the stock price for the estimated P/E ratio, which is nine.

100 divided by the ratio. Our $30 stock yields 10 percent, based on the $3 in profit during the past 12 months.

Similar ratios and yields for industry groups and market indexes are available. Investors use these indicators as benchmarks when looking at specific stocks. This approach is worthwhile because moves in these gauges over time can be substantial. The P/E for the Standard & Poor's 500 Index, displayed in Exhibit 3.11, provides an example.

Now that we have an idea how to determine relative value, it's time to look at some comparisons that help investors decide what stocks to buy, sell, or hold. This analysis can be done for individual shares or broader categories, as we saw earlier for money-market securities, notes, and bonds. Here's a summary.

History: Maybe the shares of a company are trading at record prices. Maybe they lost half their value during the past three months. Maybe they haven't changed all that much in the past three years. The only way to know is to look at historical prices, a starting point for relative-value judgments.

Historical data is available for the P/E, price-to-sales ratio, price-to-cash-flow ratio, price-to-book-value (or book) ratio and more gauges, along with dividend and earnings yields. These can shed light on the significance of price moves. If a stock has risen to a record and the P/E ratio has changed little during the past year, the price move may mean the business is doing well. If the P/E has climbed, the gain may have more to do with speculation than the company's results.

Different companies: Comparisons based on financial ratios provide the most insight when they involve shares of a company and its competitors. Dividend yields are an example. Utilities and telephone companies have the highest payouts because their businesses are stable, leaving them with plenty of money to distribute. There's little to be gained by comparing yields on a utility stock and shares of a technology company, which may be growing much faster and need cash for expansion.

Different industries: Money managers make judgments about the companies in which they invest and about the industries represented in their holdings. They may have a preference for some industry groups over others that affects their weightings, or percentage of assets. In coming to these conclusions, they look at ratios, yields, and other indicators for industry groups. They're the same as the gauges used for individual stocks except that they're based on averages.

Different categories: Industry groups are one of many ways to categorize stocks. Others include market value, growth rates, economic ties, and location. Relative-value comparisons make it possible to sort through them and determine what's worth buying, selling, or holding.

Market value is known as market capitalization (cap). Stocks can be large-cap, mid-cap, or small-cap, depending on the company's value. Some investors describe the largest companies as mega-caps and refer to the smallest as micro-caps. The dollar values used for each category depend on who's doing the categorizing

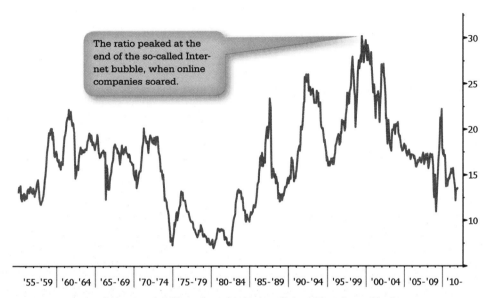

The ratio peaked at the end of the so-called Internet bubble, when online companies soared.

'55-'59 | '60-'64 | '65-'69 | '70-'74 | '75-'79 | '80-'84 | '85-'89 | '90-'94 | '95-'99 | '00-'04 | '05-'09 | '10-

Exhibit 3.11: Standard & Poor's 500 Index Price-Earnings Ratio

and how stocks are performing. It's enough to know that these breakdowns exist and can serve as a starting point for determining relative value.

Sales, earnings, assets, and other financial barometers can define companies as growth or value. Growth stocks are tied to the biggest increases in revenue and profit. Value stocks have some of the lowest price-to-book ratios. Beyond that, the criteria are as variable as the market cap thresholds. That doesn't stop investors from looking for value in one or the other.

Industries can be classified as cyclical or defensive, based on how vulnerable they are to slower economic growth and recession. Commodity, energy, industrial, and technology stocks are cyclical. Health-care, telephone, and utility shares are defensive. Consumer companies are in both categories. Cyclicals include media companies, retailers, automakers, and homebuilders, which depend on consumers' discretionary income. The makers of food, beverages, and other consumer staples are defensive stocks. By combining economic and relative-value analysis, investors can decide how heavily to bet on either category.

Location refers to countries, regions, or economic areas. The broadest distinction made globally is

KEY POINT:

Stocks are categorized by industry group and companies' market cap, short for capitalization. They can also be classified as growth or value.

between developed markets and emerging markets, as defined by the pace of economic growth and other criteria. Investors may favor one geographic region over another or concentrate on countries or markets where the outlook is most promising. These kinds of investment decisions rely on the ability to assess value worldwide, and that's made possible by the kind of analysis we have just explored.

Video:
Stock Classifications

www.wiley.com/go/bvgfinancialmarkets

Test Yourself

Answer the following multiple-choice questions:

1. The federal funds rate is set by:
   a. Banks.
   b. The Federal Reserve.
   c. The U.S. Treasury.
   d. All of the above.
   e. a and b only.
2. Companies can borrow for one year by selling:
   a. Corporate bonds.
   b. Medium-term notes.
   c. Commercial paper.
   d. All of the above.
   e. a and b only.
3. Bonds of companies with relatively low credit ratings are labeled as:
   a. Non-investment grade.
   b. High yield.
   c. Junk.
   d. All of the above.
   e. a and b only.
4. Returns on stocks always reflect:
   a. Price changes.
   b. Dividend payments.
   c. Share repurchases.
   d. All of the above.
   e. a and b only.
5. Underwriters sell:
   a. Stocks.
   b. Corporate bonds.
   c. Treasury securities.
   d. All of the above.
   e. a and b only.

Answers: 1. e; 2. b; 3. d; 4. a; 5. e

CHAPTER 4

Hard Assets

All the investments we have examined so far fit into one of three categories: stocks, bonds, and cash. Investors also can pick from a number of alternative investments, or strategies and assets other than buying stocks and bonds or holding onto cash.

Alternative can refer to hedge funds, or private partnerships that rely on investment strategies besides buying and holding securities. Private-equity funds, which acquire entire companies mainly with borrowed money, are another alternative.

We'll take a closer look at these funds and others later. For the moment, we'll focus on alternative assets. Commodities and real estate are two of the most popular types. Because of their physical presence, they're described as real assets, tangible assets, and hard assets. They are more than pieces of paper or entries on computer screens. They can protect investors against inflation risk, as their value tends to increase during periods when prices are rising more broadly.

Let's start by considering gold, a precious metal that's sometimes seen as its own asset class. This distinction exists because gold's value depends on the amount of confidence that investors have in financial assets, not just the industrial demand that matters for most raw materials.

Gold

"Do you think gold is money?"

Representative Ron Paul, a Republican from Texas, asked that question to Federal Reserve (Fed) Chairman Ben Bernanke at a congressional hearing in July 2011.

Bernanke's answer was no. "It's a precious metal," he said.

The reply prompted Paul to note that gold has been seen as money for 6,000 years. He asked, "Has somebody reversed that, eliminated that economic law?"

He then questioned why central banks owned gold and concluded, "Some people still think it's money."

This exchange shows why gold differs from other commodities. Few would argue a barrel of crude oil, a pound of copper, or a bushel of corn is money as Paul did with gold at the hearing. Yet many investors share his view of the metal's role.

Gold is often described as a store of value or a way to preserve wealth. Historically, the Fed and other central banks followed the gold standard. Their currencies were backed by the metal, resulting in what's known as hard money.

This standard has been replaced by a system of fiat money, in which currencies have value primarily because of their legal status. Fiat money has been the standard since August 1971, when the United States ended trading of gold at a fixed price of $35 an ounce. Exhibit 4.1 shows what has happened to the price.

Gold prices reflect the dollar's value because the commodity is bought and sold in dollars worldwide. They indicate the level of concern among investors about the future of the global financial system. Many investors consider gold to be a better investment than stocks, bonds, and cash during times of financial turmoil because its value extends beyond national borders. Some own gold bullion, in the form of bars or coins, to hedge against this kind of upheaval.

Bullion is called physical gold, a phrase used to distinguish the metal from the securities and derivatives linked to its value. Physical gold is a hard asset, which explains its popularity among many investors.

Individuals can own gold directly, which isn't possible for many other commodities because of the quantities and costs involved. They have the option of buying allocated gold, which banks store on behalf of the owners. There's also unallocated gold, which banks and investment funds own. Gold certificates and other securities can be backed by allocated or unallocated metal.

Central banks own gold, as Paul's questioning of Bernanke suggested. European central banks have limited gold sales under a series of five-year agreements since 1999. The International Monetary Fund (IMF), which promotes global financial stability and economic development, owns the metal as part of its official reserves for international payments.

All this means investment demand plays a larger role in setting the price of gold than it does with other commodities. Industrial demand is tied to the production of gold jewelry as well as dental fillings and electronic components.

The primary market for gold consists of sales by mining companies to their customers. Investors aren't active in that market because there aren't any initial public offerings (IPOs) for newly produced metal. Instead, they do business in secondary markets, which are split between spot and futures trading.

In spot markets, gold changes hands for immediate delivery. Buying and selling takes place over the counter. While you won't find data about the price and quantity of gold traded on a given day, market quotes are available from brokerage firms and precious-metal

DEFINITION:
Spot markets

In spot markets, gold and other commodities are sold for immediate delivery. Futures markets set prices for later deliveries.

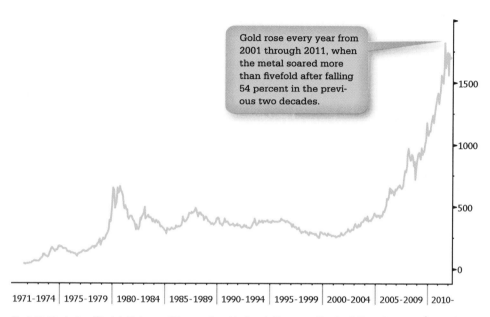

Gold rose every year from 2001 through 2011, when the metal soared more than fivefold after falling 54 percent in the previous two decades.

1500

1000

500

0

1971-1974 | 1975-1979 | 1980-1984 | 1985-1989 | 1990-1994 | 1995-1999 | 2000-2004 | 2005-2009 | 2010-

Exhibit 4.1: Gold Prices Since the United States Ended Trading at $35/Ounce

dealers. Spot prices are a benchmark for gold's market value.

Another benchmark is the London gold fixing, a price provided by a group of five dealers. The price comes from a spot market, dating back to 1919, which operates each weekday morning and afternoon. The group consists of the Barclays Capital unit of Barclays Plc, Deutsche Bank AG, HSBC Holdings Plc, Bank of Nova Scotia's ScotiaMonetta unit and Societé Generale.

Gold futures prices are followed as well. Futures contracts lock in the price for a later delivery. They trade on exchanges, which specify the amount and quality of gold as well as other contract terms. Exchanges provide data on trades as they take place. This makes the futures market easier to follow than the spot market.

As the delivery date draws closer, any price gap between gold futures and spot markets will usually shrink. There's less of a difference over time between estimates of the metal's future price, which affect the market value of the contract, and its current price.

We'll take a closer look at futures later, when we delve into derivatives. Let's focus on spot trading.

Quotations

When you look for a quote on spot gold, Exhibit 4.2 shows what you might find. Prices are quoted in dollars worldwide, which explains why the dollar sign we have seen in other quotes is missing.

GOLDS: Symbol for spot gold.

Up arrow: Uptick/downtick arrow, pointing in the direction of the latest price change.

1743.22: Price of latest trade in dollars and cents.

-39.13: Change from previous day's close. As with currencies, the market never formally closes during the week. The last trade at a specified time and place, such as 6 p.m. Eastern time in New York, represents the closing price.

DBFX: Symbol for the gold dealer with the highest bid price. In this case, it's Deutsche Bank. The FX in the symbol isn't an accident, as some of the largest securities firms have fixed income, currency, and commodity (FICC) trading desks.

1743.2/1743.25: Highest bid price, $1,743.20 an ounce, and lowest ask price, $1,743.25 an ounce.

ANON: Symbol showing the dealer with the lowest ask price has chosen to remain anonymous.

At 14:50: Time of the latest update.

Op 1782.3, Hi 1786.47, Lo 1722.03: Opening, high, and low prices for the current day.

Prev 1782.35: Closing price for the previous day, based on the specified time and place.

Three Rs

Returns are easier to figure out for gold than for stocks, bonds, and cash. Gold has no discount rate, and you can avoid any payments in the calculations. This means gold investors can't count on income they would otherwise receive. They're at the mercy of swings in spot and futures markets.

Gold's risks differ from those of financial assets. Owning the metal provides investors with insurance against extreme outcomes, according to the late Peter Bernstein, a market historian. The price of gold is the premium charged for that insurance. When investors

```
   ▲    GOLDS ↑   1743.22 -39.13   DBFX 1743.2/1743.25 ANON
   ▼    At 14:50 Op 1782.3   Hi 1786.47   Lo 1722.03   Prev 1782.35
```

Exhibit 4.2: A Spot Gold Quote

become more concerned that the outcomes might occur, the price or the premium tends to rise even as the value of stocks, bonds, and cash falls.

Relative value is less obvious with gold as well. Deciding how much an ounce of the metal should cost is more difficult than comparing prices in different markets. The kind of supply-and-demand analysis done with other commodities is less useful because of the larger role played by investment demand, which can be volatile.

Returns

Gold bullion doesn't pay interest. Gold bars don't pay dividends. Gold coins don't generate any reinvestment income. This means returns from owning bullion, bars, and coins depend on price changes.

Storage and insurance costs reduce the returns. Owners of allocated gold have to pay annual fees for keeping the metal in bank vaults and insuring against theft. These costs, along with management fees, are also borne by investors who have claims on unallocated gold.

Gold futures add more variables to the return equation as we'll touch on later. Contracts end on a regular schedule, and investors who want to maintain their bets must sell expiring contracts and buy new ones. Price differences between futures can increase or cut into returns. Investors have to keep money on deposit to own futures, and those funds earn interest.

Risks

There's a saying that every problem is an opportunity in disguise. If that's true, it might be said that gold investors see through the costume.

Risks to financial, economic, and political stability represent opportunities to make money in gold. Many investors turn to the metal as a haven from these kinds of threats. The phrase "safe haven" is often used even though a haven would be safe by definition.

Because of this tendency, growing investor confidence represents the biggest risk in owning gold. Investment demand may decline as countries and regions resolve issues that might lead to extreme outcomes.

Currency risk takes on a different meaning with gold. A stronger dollar makes the metal more costly for international investors, who must exchange their local currencies for dollars before they can make purchases. This may reduce investment demand and bring down the price.

Relative Value

Gold traded for less than $300 an ounce when the 2000s began. The market price was about $1,100 when the decade ended and approached $2,000 within the next two years. Did that surge make the precious metal too costly?

This kind of relative-value question isn't easily answered. Gold lacks a yield that can be compared with the yields on bonds or dividend paying stocks. The metal doesn't produce any revenue or earnings by sitting in a vault, so there are no price ratios to work with either.

Supply and demand figures can provide some insight. The World Gold Council, an industry trade group, presents them in quarterly reports. Gold buying is split into three categories: investment, jewelry, and technology. Even though jewelry makers are the biggest purchasers, investors have been gaining on them.

In the end, anyone trying to find out whether the metal is cheap, expensive, or fairly valued has to focus on the price of gold itself. Here are some comparisons that are worth making in the analysis.

History: The price comparisons and the chart in this chapter show that gold costs far more these days than it did when the 1990s began. The chart illustrates that a surge in the late 1970s gave way to two decades of declines. That's perspective worth having.

Other markets: Gold trades in several markets worldwide beyond the ones already mentioned. Investors with the ability to buy and sell in multiple markets can look at prices to determine where they can get the best deals. Similar opportunities may be available by comparing spot and futures prices.

Other precious metals: Silver attracts some buying from investors seeking a haven, and a ratio of gold and silver prices can serve as a guide to their decision making. The ratio show how many ounces of silver would cost as much as one ounce of gold. When gold trades at $1,800 an ounce and silver changes hands at $30, the number would be 60. Ratios can be

calculated for gold versus platinum and palladium, two other precious metals.

Commodities

China's emergence as one of the world's largest economies has bolstered demand for raw materials. Imports of steel, iron ore, coal, copper, aluminum, and other industrial products have risen as the country has gone through a building boom. Oil imports have increased as China's energy needs have grown faster than production. Corn, wheat, soybeans, and other agricultural items have been shipped in growing numbers as the Chinese standard of living increases, giving consumers more money to spend on food.

Price increases spurred by the Chinese buying have fueled growth in investment demand for commodities. Greater interest in owning assets that perform differently than stocks and bonds and protect against inflation has contributed as well. Another catalyst has been the development of new ways to invest in them, such as exchange-traded funds (ETFs), which we'll cover later.

Commodities can be split into five categories: precious metals, base or industrial metals, energy, agriculture, and livestock. Growing demand for them has led to higher prices in each category, as Exhibit 4.3 shows.

Gold fits into the precious-metal category along with silver, platinum, and palladium. The latter two metals are largely limited to industrial use. They go into catalytic converters, which reduce auto pollution, and other products.

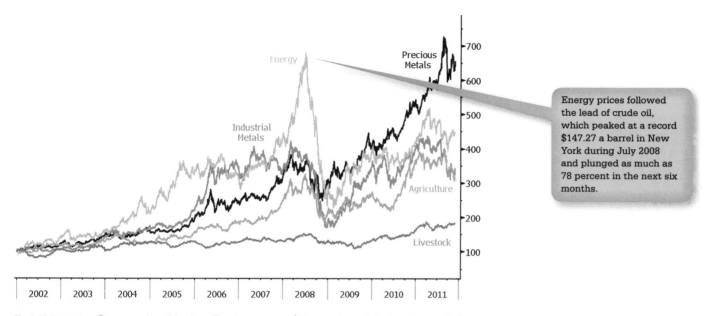

Energy prices followed the lead of crude oil, which peaked at a record $147.27 a barrel in New York during July 2008 and plunged as much as 78 percent in the next six months.

Exhibit 4.3: Commodity Market Performance (December 31, 2001 = 100)

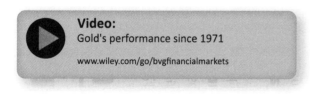

Video:
Gold's performance since 1971

www.wiley.com/go/bvgfinancialmarkets

Copper is an example of a base metal. It's sometimes described as Dr. Copper, the metal with a Ph.D. in economics, because its gains and losses are a barometer of the economy's prospects. Aluminum, lead, nickel, tin, and zinc are part of this group as well.

Crude oil dominates energy trading even though it's only part of a bigger picture. Heating oil and gasoline, two commodities made from crude, change hands actively. So do natural gas, coal, and electricity.

Grains such as corn, wheat, and soybeans are mainstays of agricultural commodity markets, as are foodstuffs, or food and beverages in raw form. Cocoa, coffee, sugar, and orange juice are all foodstuffs. The category can be stretched to include cotton, which comes from plants, and lumber, which begins with trees.

Cattle and hogs are examples of the livestock that change hands in commodity trading. Pork bellies, used to make bacon and featured in the 1983 movie "Trading Places," were in this group. Contracts on frozen bellies stopped trading in 2011 after restaurants shifted toward bacon made from fresh bellies.

All these products can be identified as commodities because they are widely available, essentially the same regardless of where they're produced, and raw materials rather than finished goods. Even gasoline is processed before it's sold at the pump.

Gold, oil wells, corn fields, or cattle herds are identical in terms of trading. The key difference in trading is between spot and futures markets, as opposed to primary and secondary markets.

Spot markets on many commodities are small and hard to follow. Base metals are one exception because there's a spot market operated by the London Metal Exchange, which reports trading data. Precious metals are another, as spot trading occurs in gold, silver, platinum, and palladium. Futures markets are more active and widely followed than spot markets as a rule. When people discuss oil prices, they're more likely to refer to New York or London futures trading than spot prices in West Texas or the North Sea, two oil-producing regions

that are closely followed. Futures can serve as price references for other commodities.

We'll concentrate on spot markets because we haven't looked at futures. When we do, we will feature commodities prominently.

Quotations

Even though spot prices for commodities aren't always benchmarks, it's worth taking a look at one that's closely tracked (see Exhibit 4.4).

The quote is for a grade of crude oil called West Texas Intermediate (WTI). It's a benchmark for oil contracts because it's plentiful, flows more easily than other grades, and is low in sulfur, which costs extra to remove.

WTI spot trading takes place over the counter, which means there's little data available. The quote is based on the price of the WTI futures contract closest to expiring, and anyone seeking a more detailed look at the market would have to focus on futures. Here are the components of the spot quote:

USCRWTIC: Symbol for WTI on the Bloomberg terminal. USCR stands for U.S. crude, as there's more than one grade. The C at the end refers to Cushing, Oklahoma, where deliveries are made.

```
  USCRWTIC  ↓80.00  -5.75   80.00/80.00
  At 13:52  Op 80.39  Hi 80.98  Lo 80.00
```

Exhibit 4.4: A West Texas Intermediate Crude-Oil Quote

Down arrow: Uptick/downtick arrow, showing the direction of the latest price change.

80.00: Latest price. There's no dollar sign included before the amount because oil, like gold, is priced in dollars worldwide.

−5.75: Change from the previous day, $5.75.

80.00/80.00: Bid and ask prices, which are the same here.

At 13:52: Time of the quote, using the 24-hour clock.

Op 80.39, Hi 80.98, Lo 80.00: Opening, high, and low prices for the current day.

Three Rs

Metals, energy, agriculture, and livestock are the same as gold from an investor's perspective. The interest payments made on notes and bonds and the dividends available from stocks are nowhere to be found. Unless the price moves the right way, the commodity investment doesn't make any money.

The risks differ because demand for commodities is tied to economic growth rather than instability. There's a greater need for metals used in buildings, machinery, cars, appliances, electronics, and other products as the economy accelerates. Oil, natural gas, and other forms of energy provide the power to keep them running. Grains, meats, and other foods gain popularity as household income increases, especially in emerging markets.

Additionally, you can assess relative value in commodities in ways that are less relevant for gold. Investors can look at whether to sell them now or to store them for sale later. They can compare the cost of raw materials, such as crude oil, with the price of products to gauge processing profits.

Returns

Chances are that no one will offer a chance to buy 1,000 barrels of crude oil unless you're an institutional investor, a brokerage, or an energy company. Let's suspend disbelief for a moment and pretend the opportunity arose.

Assuming you made the deal, changes in the price of crude would determine if you turned a profit. Any gain would have to exceed storage and transportation costs for the oil, along with trading fees and expenses.

Returns for commodity futures work the same way as those for gold futures, so price changes aren't the whole story. Many investors sell contracts as the expiration date approaches and buy contracts that mature at a later date. This process is called a **futures roll**, and we'll learn more about it when we focus on futures. For now, it's enough to know that the price gap between contracts has an effect on returns.

Interest on deposits has to be accounted for. The funds, known as margins, vary from one contract to the next. We'll revisit them in our look at futures.

> **DEFINITION:**
> **Futures roll**
>
> In a futures roll, traders sell contracts about to come due and buy contracts with a later expiration date.

Risks

Economic risk stands out as a concern for commodity investors as noted earlier. These days, the biggest risk is related to the Chinese economy. China is the world's largest buyer of many commodities, and slower growth in the country could send shock waves through markets for raw materials.

Market and liquidity risks are present, especially for investors owning commodities rather than futures. There may be less demand for 1,000 barrels of oil than for a contract on the same amount of crude. The oil buyer would have to take delivery, unlike the futures buyer, who can sell the contract later without owning the crude.

Commodity investors have to be mindful of event risk. Floods, droughts, and other natural disasters can cause price swings, tied to changes in supply. Shipping lane closures, pipeline breakdowns, and refinery shutdowns can have the same effect.

Relative Value

Commodities offer more opportunity to analyze what's cheap, expensive, or fairly priced than gold if only because more than one product is available to consider. Each has its own balance of supply and demand, which can be tracked through industry data. For instance, U.S. government statistics influence prices for energy, farm products, and livestock.

Though equivalents for bond yields and stock price ratios are unavailable, that's less of an issue than it was for gold. Prices and price moves can be more telling, as you'll see from these possible comparisons.

History: Energy soared far more than other commodities during the 2000s and tumbled before the end of the decade, as the chart in this chapter shows. Precious metals ended up in a similar position more recently. Anyone making the comparison might conclude that history would repeat itself, a signal that gold and other precious metals were too expensive. That's the kind of insight available from studying past pricing.

Other markets: Oil, like gold, is traded around the world. Though crude varies more than gold in its makeup, investors can make judgments about relative value that account for those differences. As a price gap between two grades of crude widens or narrows, one or the other may become cheap. That happened in 2011 with WTI, a benchmark for U.S. trading, as Exhibit 4.5 illustrates. WTI changed hands for about $28 a barrel less than its European counterpart, North Sea Brent (Brent), during the year as shipments failed to keep pace with production.

Similar commodities: Five categories were defined in the chart. It's possible to split grains from food and fiber, namely cotton, in the agricultural products group. Prices for the commodities within each group provide a basis for making buying and selling decisions.

Raw material versus products: Oil markets have crack spreads. Crack refers to a catalytic cracker, a

---

KEY POINT:

Like gold, oil is priced in dollars worldwide. This means WTI and Brent can be compared directly even though Brent is produced in a region where the dollar isn't the local currency.

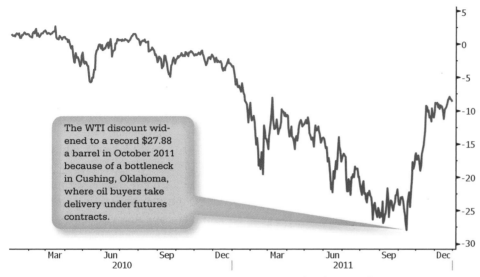

The WTI discount widened to a record $27.88 a barrel in October 2011 because of a bottleneck in Cushing, Oklahoma, where oil buyers take delivery under futures contracts.

Exhibit 4.5: Price Gap between WTI and Brent (in $/barrel)

piece of refining equipment that turns crude into gasoline, heating oil, and other products. Spreads track the difference between the cost of crude and the market price of the products, a gauge of relative value. Refiners make more money when these spreads widen and less when they narrow. Similarly, crush spreads compare the cost of soybeans with the price of soybean oil and soybean meal, produced by crushing the beans.

Real Estate

Yale University's endowment fund became a model for its peers by making investments well beyond stocks,

bonds, and money market securities. Under David Swensen, who was named chief investment officer in 1985, the endowment posted an average annual return of 13.1 percent for the 20 years ending in June 2010.

Near the end of the period, the fund had the biggest chunk of its money in "real assets," as defined in financial reports. Oil and gas fields and farmland, which benefited from commodity price increases, were among them. There was also real estate.

When Yale's endowment and other institutional investors put money into real estate, they have two choices at their disposal. First, they can buy properties themselves, hire managers to run them, and earn the income they produce. Second, they can invest in real estate funds and leave all the work to the fund manager.

Most individual investors don't have the same kinds of opportunities because the price tag for real estate is too high. They might be able to buy a home or two and rent them, but that's about it. Real estate funds are a less costly investment along with real estate investment trusts (REITs), which are specifically created to own property and are governed by different rules than the average company.

We'll look at REITs more closely later, when we revisit the investments covered so far. For now, let's focus directly on the real estate.

There are three main types of investment properties: commercial, residential, and land. Shopping malls and stores, office buildings, warehouses, self-storage facilities, hotels and motels, and hospitals are examples of commercial real estate. Apartment buildings are in the residential category along with mobile home parks. The oil and gas fields and farms that Yale's endowment fund owns take their place alongside timberland, mine sites, and undeveloped land as investment choices.

The value of commercial property has much to do with the economy's performance. When consumers are spending more, the value of the places where they make purchases is likely to rise. When corporate profits are increasing, companies are more likely to expand, which means they may have to add office and warehouse space. They are more likely to send

employees on business trips, benefiting the hotel and motel industry.

U.S. commercial real estate values went through a bigger boom and bust than home prices in the 2000s and beyond, as the chart below shows. The swings in commercial prices are reflected in an index from Moody's Investors Service and another company, Real Estate Analytics LLC. The housing index comes from S&P, working with economists Robert Shiller and Karl Case (see Exhibit 4.6).

Though economic growth influences residential real estate values, the two don't move in tandem. Demand for rental housing may rise when the economy falters because fewer people can afford to buy homes. This was the case during the 2007–2009 recession and its aftermath, a period in which apartment demand rose as falling house prices deterred many potential buyers.

Land values mirror the economy more closely because the pace of growth influences the value of the commodities produced there. The housing bubble that ended in 2007 meant higher prices for lumber and the timberland where the wood came from. China's increasing demand for crop imports has had a similar effect on farmland. Higher energy and metals prices have meant rising values for oil and gas leases and mining rights.

The primary market for real estate is composed of sales, leases, and rentals that property developers make. When a building or piece of land gets bought, the purchase takes place in the secondary market.

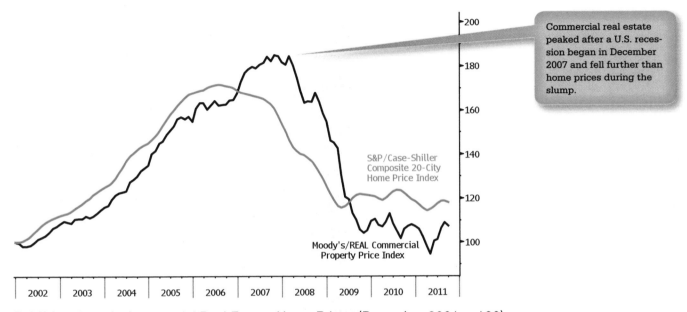

> Commercial real estate peaked after a U.S. recession began in December 2007 and fell further than home prices during the slump.

S&P/Case-Shiller Composite 20-City Home Price Index

Moody's/REAL Commercial Property Price Index

Exhibit 4.6: U.S. Commercial Real Estate, Home Prices (December 2001 = 100)

Specific properties seldom change hands, and there isn't an exchange where they are bought and sold. Instead, real estate brokers line up property listings and work with potential purchasers to arrange sales. Investment banks take the place of brokers for more costly deals.

Quotations

Price quotes on real estate are about as simple as it gets. They consist of an offer price, which is the dollar amount that a seller wants for the property.

There are no symbols, market prices, volume figures, or any other details we have become used to seeing for securities. Properties don't change hands often enough to generate those kinds of data.

Three Rs

When we looked at notes and bonds earlier, we saw yield was a common denominator for deciding what was cheap, expensive, and fairly valued. Real estate has a similar gauge, known as capitalization (cap) rates.

Cap rates indicate how much an investor stands to earn on a property. They're based on income, operating expenses, and purchase prices. Only purchase prices are fixed, which means the rates may be more volatile than bond yields. We'll see how they're put together shortly.

Real estate owners face the same kind of business-related risks as holders of a company's debt and equity. They must make relative-value judgments, complicated by a lack of publicly available data. Let's spend some time looking at how the three Rs apply to them.

Returns

As yields are a starting point for note and bond returns, cap rates show the potential gains from real estate. They provide a way to evaluate properties and to determine if deals are worth doing or avoiding.

Cap rate calculations begin with rent or lease payments, depending on the type of building. For example, let's consider a shopping center that receives $12,000 a month from the retail stores located there. Multiply the amount by 12 and you end up with $144,000 a year in income.

We have to subtract the costs of maintenance, repairs, and other expenses of running the building. Let's assume they totaled $24,000 for the latest year. Subtract that amount and we're left with $120,000, which real estate investors would define as net operating income.

There's one more detail to add to this scenario: the property is up for sale with a $1.5 million asking price. Prospective buyers would have to evaluate its worth.

As part of that process, they would want to know how much they stand to make on the deal.

Cap rates indicate what's possible. The rate for our example is 8 percent, or $120,000 divided by $1.5 million. If a buyer pays less for the shopping center, the rate will increase accordingly. If multiple bidders are competing and the price rises, the rate will drop. The relationship is the same as the link we saw earlier between note and bond prices and yields.

Differences between cap rates and yields exist that are worth noting. Net operating income isn't guaranteed. Next year's earnings may decline as retailers close and stores go unoccupied, or as maintenance costs pile up. Either of these events would reduce the cap rate. On the other hand, income may increase as store leases expire and the owner raises rates. The cap rate would rise accordingly.

The 8 percent figure may not be comparable to cap rates for other shopping centers. Data used to calculate the rates often aren't publicly available, and accounting differences among property owners may affect the results. Less room for discrepancies is available with 10-year note yields, for instance, as security prices and payment amounts can be verified.

Financing costs are another variable to consider though they weren't included in our example. The 8 percent figure assumed the buyer paid cash for the property, which is seldom done. Any interest expense on debt would have to be subtracted from net operating income to calculate returns.

Risks

When we revisit the first level of risks, we can see two significant ones for investors in real estate. Liquidity risk is relatively high because offices, apartments, and other buildings often carry price tags in the millions of dollars and can take months or years to sell. Economic risk is an issue for owners of commercial properties, as their success in finding tenants and producing income depends on how well businesses are performing.

Business risk, event risk, and industry risk apply. Real estate investors may end up with properties that are less lucrative or are in less desirable locations, as the market changes over time. Disputes may occur with leaseholders or tenants that result in lost payments and legal costs.

Fires, floods, and other disasters can destroy and damage buildings, which reduces income and increases expenses at the same time. And when the industry takes a turn for the worse, there's plenty of suffering to go around, as Exhibit 4.6 makes clear.

Relative Value

The similarity between cap rates and note and bond yields carries over to their use in evaluating what's cheap, expensive, or fairly priced. Comparing rates is similar to studying yield spreads. The higher the rate, the more value there may be in a property, and vice versa.

Cap rates provide a way to compare returns on real estate and other types of investments. Blackstone Group LP carried out a $39 billion buyout of Equity Office Properties at a 5.3 percent cap rate, as noted in a February 2007 story from Bloomberg News. That was a record low, according to Green Street Advisors Inc., a research firm that came up with the figure. Ten-year Treasury notes yielded about 4.7 percent, which indicated the additional return on the deal was only about 0.6 percentage point.

Even so, this analysis has limits. Cap rates aren't turned into the equivalent of yield curves as the time element isn't the same. Instead of maturity dates, the timing of deals matters. More recent sales are usually a better gauge of value than those completed months earlier, when the real estate market may have differed.

To address the issue, brokers and investment banks obtain data on comparable properties (comps) that have changed hands. Looking at the comps helps the firms set selling prices along with aiding potential buyers.

Replacement value and income potential provide a basis for judging if real estate is worth buying. The first gauge is based on the projected cost of a new building that's similar to the one being sold. The second focuses on how much money the property could generate, as opposed to the current income.

Test Yourself

Answer the following multiple-choice questions:

1. Investors seeking to own gold can buy:
   a. Jewelry.
   b. Bullion.
   c. Futures.
   d. All of the above.
   e. a and b only.

2. These organizations own gold:
   a. The Federal Reserve.
   b. The World Bank.
   c. The United Nations.
   d. All of the above.
   e. a and b only.

3. The benchmark grade of U.S. crude oil is commonly called:
   a. USCR.
   b. WTI.
   c. Brent.
   d. All of the above.
   e. a and b only.

4. Commodity-related properties that investors can buy include:
   a. Farms.
   b. Timberland.
   c. Oil and gas fields.
   d. All of the above.
   e. a and b only.

5. Cap-rate calculations for real estate exclude:
   a. Rental income.
   b. Maintenance costs.
   c. Interest payments.
   d. All of the above.
   e. a and b only.

Answers: 1. d; 2. e; 3. b; 4. d; 5. c

CHAPTER 5

Indexes

The 2000s have been called a lost decade for U.S. stock investors because they lost money even after taking dividends into account. Exhibit 5.1 shows how stocks fared relative to the dollar, bonds, commodities, and real estate in the 10-year period.

This kind of comparison is made possible by market indexes, which track performance over time. Indexes provide a way to gauge the daily performance of currency, debt, equity, and hard asset markets and a way to assess their moves during the day.

Each market has indicators that provide more specific data. Stock indexes, for example, can be used to compare larger companies with those that are mid-sized and smaller. They track industry groups and other market segments.

Money managers use indexes to show whether they're beating the market. Funds specializing in the largest U.S. companies may focus on how their returns compare with those of the Standard & Poor's 500 Index, a gauge of similar stocks. Bond funds may use debt indexes for the same purpose.

Indexes provide a basis for the derivatives and funds that we'll come across in looking at indirect investing. Various contracts are tied to an index's value, and hundreds of funds are designed to mirror a benchmark's moves.

Put another way, indexes let you follow markets and provide a way for you to invest in them. This dual purpose is more than enough reason to take a closer look at these indicators.

Currency

When people talk about a weaker or stronger dollar, they might be referring to another specific currency, like the yen. In many cases, they're talking about a gain or loss of value against a number of currencies.

Indexes are the easiest way to track the broader moves. Exhibit 5.2 compares the performance of three indicators during the 2000s.

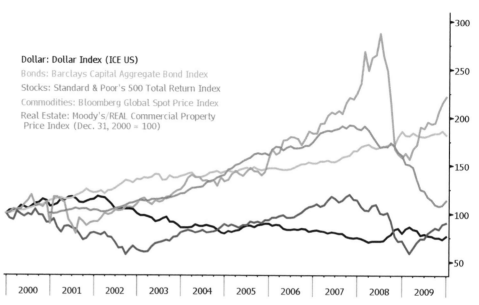

Dollar: Dollar Index (ICE US)
Bonds: Barclays Capital Aggregate Bond Index
Stocks: Standard & Poor's 500 Total Return Index
Commodities: Bloomberg Global Spot Price Index
Real Estate: Moody's/REAL Commercial Property
Price Index (Dec. 31, 2000 = 100)

Exhibit 5.1: Market Performance during the 2000s (December 31, 1999 = 100)

DEFINITION:
Trade-weighted indexes

A trade-weighted index is based on the value of a country's currency against several others. Each currency's weighting in the index is tied to the share of trade with the country.

The Dollar Index is among them. The indicator, calculated by the IntercontinentalExchange (ICE), is based on the value of the U.S. currency against the euro, Japanese yen, British pound, Canadian dollar, Swedish krona, and Swiss franc.

Trade is taken into account in determining each currency's share of the index. The euro accounts for more than half of its value. That's based on the amount of imports and exports moving between the United States and countries using the European currency.

Two trade-weighted indexes are compiled by the Federal Reserve (Fed). One of them shows the dollar's value against major currencies, defined by the Fed as the Australian dollar and the components of the Dollar Index. The other is broader, including the Chinese yuan, Mexican peso. and other emerging market currencies.

These indexes, and others compiled by firms such as Barclays Capital and Goldman Sachs, are based on the dollar's swings against other currencies. Deposit rates, mentioned earlier as an influence on investment returns, aren't part of the calculations.

The dollar held onto more value in the currency market against smaller countries than the U.S.'s main trading partners.

Broad Dollar Index, Trade Weighted

Major Currency Dollar Index, Trade Weighted

Dollar Index

Exhibit 5.2: Currency Index Performance (December 31, 1999 = 100)
Sources: ICE US, Federal Reserve, Bloomberg.

Debt

Lending money to governments and companies produced the kinds of returns in the 2000s that were associated with stocks in past decades. Exhibit 5.3 shows the relative performance of government debt, corporate debt, mortgage-backed debt, and municipal debt, as well as Treasury bills, during the 10-year period.

In Exhibit 5.3, the four bond indexes were relatively close to each other when a crisis began to sweep through the financial system in 2007. At that point,

many investors bought Treasury securities for their relative safety and sold riskier types of debt, especially corporate securities.

It's worth noting that these indexes weren't provided by exchanges, which play a minor role in bond trading. The government bond indicator is compiled by Bloomberg, along with the European Federation of Financial Analysts Societies (EFFAS), a regional trade group.

The corporate, mortgage, and municipal indexes come from Barclays Capital, a unit of Barclays Plc that's among the biggest dealers in U.S. bonds.

KEY POINT:

Indexes can track price changes or total returns, which include interest or dividend income. Bond benchmarks reflect returns, while the most widely followed stock-market indicators are price-based.

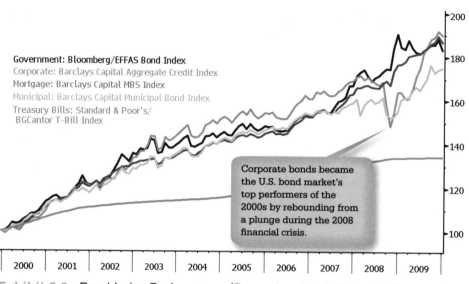

Government: Bloomberg/EFFAS Bond Index
Corporate: Barclays Capital Aggregate Credit Index
Mortgage: Barclays Capital MBS Index
Municipal: Barclays Capital Municipal Bond Index
Treasury Bills: Standard & Poor's/
BGCantor T-Bill Index

> Corporate bonds became the U.S. bond market's top performers of the 2000s by rebounding from a plunge during the 2008 financial crisis.

Exhibit 5.3: Bond Index Performance (December 31, 1999 = 100)

The Treasury-bill index is from Standard & Poor's and a market data unit of BGC Partners Inc., a bond broker.

BGC is a recent entrant into the world of bond data, as the bill index made its debut in March 2010. The Barclays Capital indicators have been around for longer, as they were produced by Lehman Brothers Holdings Inc. before that firm went into bankruptcy in September 2008.

Bond indexes from securities firms have traditionally served as market benchmarks. Bank of America Corp.'s Merrill Lynch unit and JPMorgan Chase & Co. are among the providers of index series similar to Barclays Capital's.

S&P and other independent providers compile bond indexes as well. Bloomberg produces gauges for Treasuries and government bonds in 25 other countries through an agreement with EFFAS.

Regardless of who puts them together and calculates their value, bond indexes are based on total returns, which account for interest payments and price changes. This feature sets them apart from the most widely followed stock indexes.

Other indexes track the average yield spread between a specific category of bonds and U.S. Treasuries. These are called **option-adjusted spreads (OAS)** because they account for the value of any options built

DEFINITION:
Option-adjusted spreads

Option-adjusted spreads (OAS) exclude the estimated value of options to call, put, or convert individual securities. They are used to calculate some bond indexes.

into the bonds. A borrower might be able to buy back the debt before maturity at a set price, or an owner may be able to sell it back the same way. Taking them out of the equation ensures the bonds are comparable to each other.

Indexes may focus on bond-market segments, especially for government debt. The Bloomberg and EFFAS indexes, for instance, break down Treasury bills, notes, and bonds into six categories based on the amount of time to maturity. There are indexes for securities maturing in less than a year, 1 to 3 years, 3 to 5 years, 5 to 7 years, 7 to 10 years, and more than 10 years.

Equity

U.S. stock-market reports in newspapers, online, and on radio and television cite three indexes as a matter of course. They are the Dow Jones Industrial Average (DJIA or Dow), the Standard & Poor's 500 Index, and the NASDAQ Composite Index.

The Dow average is the oldest of these indicators. It has been calculated since 1896 and has been composed of 30 stocks since 1928. The average's members are among the biggest U.S. companies. Not all of them are industrials these days as financial stocks are included.

Standard & Poor's introduced the S&P 500 in 1957, and data for the index go back to 1928. The S&P 500 tracks more of the largest U.S. companies than the Dow industrials and is more widely used as a gauge of money managers' performance. Funds with trillions

of dollars in assets use the S&P 500 as a benchmark. Some are created specifically to mirror the index, and we'll learn more about them later.

The NASDAQ Composite tracks all of the shares listed on the NASDAQ Stock Market. Technology companies account for the bulk of its value. Two of the biggest ones are Microsoft Corp. and Intel Corp., which became the first NASDAQ companies to join the Dow industrials in 1999.

Exhibit 5.4 shows how the lost decade of the 2000s looked for each of the three indicators.

Stock indexes can be defined by three criteria, starting with their coverage. The Dow industrials and the S&P 500 cover the entire U.S. market, but the NASDAQ Composite is tied to a specific exchange.

Other indexes focus on market segments. The Russell 2000 Index, compiled by Russell Investments, is a good example. The Russell 2000 is a popular indicator for small-cap companies, which have less market value than those in the Dow average or the S&P 500.

S&P has four levels of indexes that track industry groups. The broadest consists of 10 categories, including two for consumer-related companies. Energy, financial, health care, industrial, raw material, technology, and telephone and utility companies round out the lineup. The narrowest has about 130 industries, including some that consist of only one or two companies.

The second criteria is the method of weighting or determining each stock's effect on the value of an index. Share prices are used for the Dow industrials. The

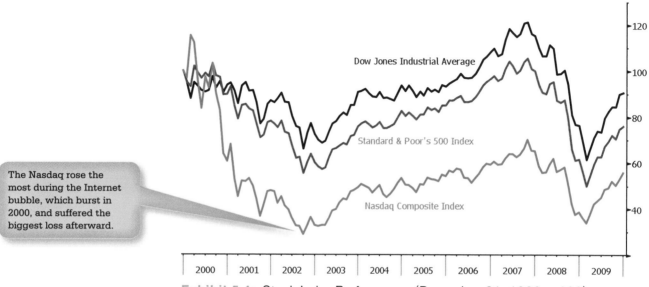

The Nasdaq rose the most during the Internet bubble, which burst in 2000, and suffered the biggest loss afterward.

Exhibit 5.4: Stock Index Performance (December 31, 1999 = 100)

company whose stock costs the most to buy counts the most in the average, and vice versa. Company size doesn't matter, so the smallest member of the average could have the biggest effect on its performance.

Weighting stocks by market capitalization (market cap) addresses the size issue. The S&P 500 was calculated this way, and the NASDAQ Composite still is. A drawback emerged as funds made greater use of indexes to gauge their performance and guide their trading. Their decision making was influenced by shares they couldn't buy because insiders and major investors owned them. Those shares counted toward market value even though they were off the market.

Index providers resolved this concern by using float, or the number of shares available for trading, in place of market cap to weight each company. The S&P 500 became a float-adjusted index, and others followed.

These changes weren't enough to please everyone. Another method was developed that took market value out of the equation entirely. Robert Arnott, the founder of the Research Affiliates LLC investment firm, created indexes that weighed companies by sales, earnings, dividends, and other company-specific gauges. Arnott's approach, fundamental indexing, reflects his view that a company's market value is often out of line with the performance of its business.

Finally, there's the role of dividends. The most popular stock indexes are based only on price changes as a rule. This means they can't be compared directly with bond indexes, which include interest payments. To overcome this hurdle, stock index providers compile total return versions of their indicators.

Hard Assets

Although gold, commodities, and real estate are similar because of their hard-asset status, their markets differ. Indexes that track them all aren't readily available. Exhibit 5.5 shows each one separately by comparing gold with commodity and real estate indexes.

Gold's spot price plays the role of an index in the chart. That's the case in the precious metals market, where it's a widely followed benchmark.

Commodities are represented by the Bloomberg Spot Commodity Index, based on price quotes on 24 raw materials for immediate delivery. They are divided into six categories, including energy, precious metals,

> **KEY POINT:**
>
> **The three main benchmarks for U.S. stocks are each calculated differently. The Dow average is price weighted, the S&P 500 is float weighted, and the Nasdaq Composite is market-cap weighted.**

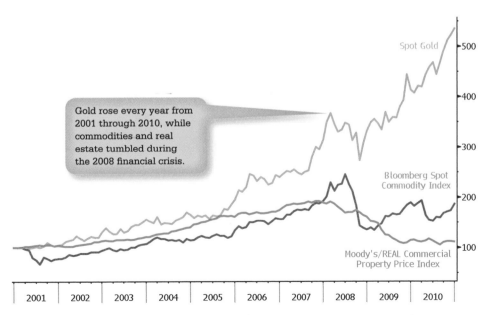

Gold rose every year from 2001 through 2010, while commodities and real estate tumbled during the 2008 financial crisis.

Exhibit 5.5: Hard Asset Performance (December 31, 2000 = 100)

and base metals. Corn, soybeans, and wheat comprise the crops category. Sugar, coffee, cocoa, and cotton are classified as food and fiber. A livestock group consists of steers and hogs.

Other commodity gauges that are called spot indexes are based on futures prices. For those indicators, "spot" refers to market performance, the main component of total returns. Other sources of returns are included in some commodity futures indexes as we'll learn when we examine indexes based on derivatives.

The Moody's/REAL index represents commercial real estate. Moody's and Real Estate Analytics work with two other organizations on the index. The data are compiled by Real Capital Analytics Inc., and the methodology comes from the Massachusetts Institute of Technology's Center for Real Estate.

Moody's publishes the index, based on sale prices, every month. Indicators for apartments, offices, industrial buildings, and retail stores are available every quarter. There are gauges for metropolitan areas as well.

Quarterly indexes are also available from the National Council of Real Estate Investment Fiduciaries (NCREIF), a trade group that serves institutional investors. The council tracks farmland and timberland prices and the performance of private equity funds specializing in real estate.

CHAPTER 6

Government Revisited

U.S. Treasuries are a mainstay of the government bond market for a few reasons. Trillions of dollars' worth of bills, notes, and bonds are outstanding, which makes an abundance of securities available for trading. The newest ones are bought and sold more often than other types of bonds. They change hands minute by minute, let alone day by day. Finally, Treasuries are sold in dollars, the world's reserve currency. This increases their appeal for central banks and others who want the safest places to invest their money.

Yet the market extends far beyond Treasuries. Supranational borrowers play a role in public finance by raising funds on behalf of global and regional organizations. Countries around the world rely on bond investors to help pay their bills. U.S. government agencies sell bills, notes, and bonds, and they are an alternative to Treasury securities. U.S. state and local governments borrow in the bond market as well.

The World Bank, which provides financing and technical support for development projects in emerging markets worldwide, sells bonds through the International Bank for Reconstruction and Development and the International Finance Corp., a private lending unit. The European Investment Bank and the Asian Development Bank play similar roles in their regions with funding obtained from bond investors.

The European sovereign debt crisis that surfaced in 2011 drove home the reliance of governments across the region on bond financing. In Japan, yields on 10-year government debt dropped below 2 percent years before 10-year Treasuries made a similar move. Australia, Canada, other developed countries, and a number of emerging markets sell government bonds as well.

The two largest providers of U.S. mortgage financing, the Federal National Mortgage Association (FNMA or Fannie Mae) and the Federal Home Loan

> **DEFINITION:**
> **Supranational**
>
> Supranational borrowers are global organizations, such as the World Bank, or regional groups, such as the European Investment Bank, that are backed by a number of governments.

Mortgage Corp. (FHLMC or Freddie Mac), regularly sell bills, notes, and bonds to raise funds for home loan purchases from banks and other lenders. Fannie Mae taps the money market through Benchmark Bills, coming due in three, six, and 12 months. Freddie Mac follows suit through sales of Reference Bills. Both sell Discount Notes, with maturities ranging from overnight to 360 days.

Fannie Mae sells notes and bonds under the Benchmark name as well. Freddie Mac does the same with the Reference name and raises additional funds by selling medium-term notes (MTNs). As if this wasn't enough, they sell securities backed by home loans, which we'll examine in more detail later in this chapter.

Government bond investors can choose from securities sold by the Federal Home Loan Bank System, which helps finance local banks and credit unions; the Federal Farm Credit Banks, which support lenders in agricultural and rural areas; and the Tennessee Valley Authority (TVA), which provides electricity in seven Southern states.

Why lend money to U.S. agencies, other countries, or the World Bank rather than buying Treasuries? Yield is part of the equation. Many of these securities have higher potential returns than U.S. government debt, as a yield curve comparison between agency bills, notes, and bonds and Treasuries shows (see Exhibit 6.1).

Buying non-U.S. government debt can reduce currency risk. Though many countries sell dollar-denominated bonds, they raise funds in local currencies as well. When those currencies rise in value against the dollar, the interest and principal payments on the debt are worth more to U.S. investors.

Otherwise, the risks of investing in these variations on government debt are similar to those we examined earlier with Treasuries. The biggest difference is that global and regional organizations, other countries, and government agencies may lack the kind of taxing power and money printing capability that the United States has at its disposal. This means the financial backing for their securities may not be as solid.

Now that we have surveyed these securities, let's take a closer look at two categories. We'll begin with municipal bonds, which U.S. state and local governments sell to fill budget gaps and pay for public projects. Then we'll examine mortgage-backed securities (MBS), which enable Fannie Mae, Freddie Mac, and banks to repackage home loans and sell them to investors.

Municipal Bonds

The finances of U.S. state and local government borrowers emerged as a national issue in December 2010 after Meredith Whitney, an analyst at her own securities firm, sounded an alarm on the CBS television show *60 Minutes*. Her views had an impact because she had forecasted three years earlier, before a crisis shook the U.S. financial system, that Citigroup Inc.

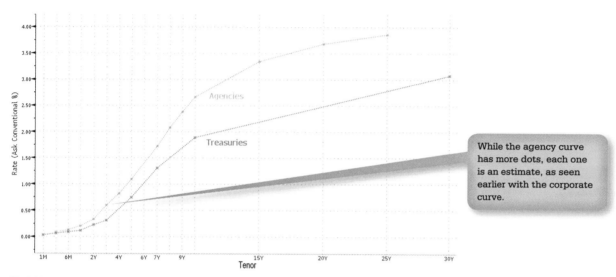

While the agency curve has more dots, each one is an estimate, as seen earlier with the corporate curve.

Exhibit 6.1: U.S. Government Agency and Treasury Yield Curve

would have to cut its dividend or sell assets to raise capital.

"There's not a doubt in my mind that you will see a spate of municipal-bond defaults," Whitney said during the interview. She described a spate as "50 to 100 sizeable defaults, more. This will amount to hundreds of billions of dollars."

Less than a year after her appearance, the largest municipal bankruptcy in U.S. history took place in Jefferson County, Alabama, where the city of Birmingham is located. The county filed for court protection in November 2011. Central Falls, Rhode Island, made

a similar petition earlier in the year. Harrisburg, Pennsylvania, sought bankruptcy as well, though its initial filing was rejected because the city didn't have state authorization. Even so, the number of defaults during the first nine months of 2011 fell by about half from the same period a year earlier, according to figures compiled by the Distressed Debt Securities Newsletter. In dollar terms, the decline was steeper at about two-thirds.

Statistics for the three decades leading up to Jefferson County's filing offered a starker contrast. Fewer than 40 local governments asked for bankruptcy protection, according to court records compiled by Bloomberg News. The number of filings made by companies was more than 20,000.

The relative safety of municipal bonds, which help states, counties, cities, and their agencies meet daily financing needs and pay for public projects, explains their appeal to many investors. Some borrowers enhance the safety of their debt through arrangements with bond-insurance companies, which make interest and principal payments if the borrowers can't.

Municipal debt can provide income that's exempt from federal, state, and local taxes. The value of these tax-free earnings varies with an investor's tax bracket. Residents of states with high income tax rates, such as California and New York, have more of an incentive to buy these bonds than people living in Florida, Texas, and other states that don't impose income taxes.

Regardless of the tax benefits, municipal bonds fit into one of two categories. General obligation bonds (GOs) are similar to Treasuries because they are backed by the power to impose and raise taxes. The municipality or municipal agency that sells them is responsible for making the payments. Revenue bonds are used to finance the construction of sewer treatment plants, toll roads, and other projects. Payments on these securities are made only from the revenue these facilities generate.

The primary market for state and local government debt can be divided in two. In competitive sales, which are similar to Treasury auctions, brokerages compete to purchase the securities for resale to investors. The firm that delivers the best deal for the borrower wins.

In negotiated sales, the borrower selects the securities firm and works out the terms in advance. Some governments have standing relationships with an individual firm, which arranges sales as they arise and promotes the bonds to customers. These ties are governed by pay-to-play rules, designed to prevent firms from winning bond business by making political donations.

Many municipal bond issues never reach the secondary market because they're bought and held until maturity. Those that are traded change hands over the counter, in an electronic market with millions of listings. Only a relative handful of bonds trade actively.

Quotations

Let's look at a bond from California, one of those high-income-tax states, as an example. The state sold $1.2 billion of the bonds in 2009 as part of the biggest tax-exempt borrowing in five years. Yet a market price isn't available for the securities (see Exhibit 6.2).

CA ST -CA 6 4/ 1/2038 112.4 (4.054)BFV

Exhibit 6.2: A California Municipal-Bond Quote

CA ST: Abbreviation for the state of California.

CA: Two-letter state code.

6: Annual interest rate of 6 percent.

4/1/2038: Maturity date.

112.4: Current price as a percentage of face value.

4.054: Tax-free yield, in percent, at the current price.

BFV: Bloomberg Fair Value, the source of the price and yield. As we saw previously with the Security Capital bond, BFV is an estimate based on the bond's terms, the maturity date, the borrower's credit rating, and other criteria.

Three Rs

Most municipal bonds have two yields. A tax-free yield is based on the purchase price and interest rate, like yields on other debt securities. A taxable-equivalent yield adjusts for tax savings that go along with owning the bonds.

Taxable-equivalent yields can be as much as 46 percent higher, based on the current federal and state income-tax brackets. The exact percentage depends on the location of the bond seller and investor and the security's tax status.

Tax benefits influence all of the three Rs. They have to be accounted for when calculating returns and making relative-value comparisons. They pose a risk because lawmakers can reduce or eliminate them through tax law changes.

Returns

State and local governments are able to raise funds more cheaply because of the tax exemptions available on their bonds. The California bonds quoted earlier are an example because interest isn't subject to state and federal taxes.

The tax-free yield of 4.05 percent on the debt amounts to a taxable-equivalent yield of about 6.25 percent, based on the U.S. exemption and the country's top income tax rate of 35 percent.

California is among 41 states that impose an income tax on its residents. The state's top bracket is 9.3 percent, and anyone who has a million-dollar income has to pay another 1 percent. That adds up to 10.3 percent. For anyone paying the state's top rate, the bonds have a taxable-equivalent yield of about 7.4 percent.

Two other states, New Hampshire and Tennessee, tax only interest and dividend income. This means residents are eligible for benefits similar to those available in California by buying municipal debt. Alaska, Florida, Nevada, South Dakota, Texas, Washington, and Wyoming have no income tax at all.

Not all municipal bonds are tax-free. Taxable securities are sold to pay for sports arenas and other projects that are ineligible for tax-exempt financing under federal regulations. Governments sold subsidized taxable debt in the Build America Bonds program, which lasted from April 2009 to December 2010. Federal subsidies covered 35 percent of the interest expense.

STEP-BY-STEP: TAXABLE EQUIVALENT YIELD

1. Assume a municipal bond has a tax-free yield of 3 percent.
2. Determine the investor's federal tax bracket. We'll use 35 percent.
3. Determine the investor's state tax bracket, assuming the bond was sold by a state or local government or agency. We'll use 10 percent.
4. Add the federal and state brackets for the overall tax rate. Here, it's 45 percent.
5. Divide the tax-free yield by 1 minus the tax rate for a taxable-equivalent yield, as in 3/(1 − 0.45) = 5.45 percent

KEY POINT:

Tax benefits available to municipal-bond investors are based on state income-tax brackets and other laws, and vary from state to state.

Yields on taxable notes and bonds are comparable to those on Treasuries and corporate securities. They are based on the debt's price relative to face value, the interest rate, and the payment schedule. Taxable debt is aimed at investors who can't benefit from owning tax-free securities. Mutual funds, insurers, and non-U.S. investors are among them.

Risks

The risks that go along with owning government and corporate bills, notes, and bonds depend on who's doing the borrowing and where the money's going. Even though this is true for municipal bonds as well, both questions have to be answered to define these risks.

States, counties, cities, and other municipalities sell GOs. All the tax revenue they don't collect for a specific reason is available to pay interest and repay principal on the GOs. The pace of economic growth and the influence of politics and policy can cause revenue to decline, hampering the government's ability to make payments.

Governments sell revenue bonds through agencies and other entities that are created for specific projects. These entities, rather than the government, are responsible for making payments on the debt. Investors face greater risk than they do with GOs because the project's revenue has to cover the expense. If it doesn't, they won't be able to legally ask the government to pay.

GOs and revenue bonds can be tax-exempt, which means tax policy is a more general risk for municipal

investors. The risk turned into reality for Florida residents in 2007 when the state repealed a tax on intangible personal property, including municipal bonds. The state doesn't have an income tax, so the repeal eliminated the tax benefit from owning bonds sold by state and local governments.

Relative Value

Yield curves and spreads are available for municipal debt as they are with government and corporate bills, notes, and bonds. They provide a way to determine which securities are cheap, expensive, or fairly valued,

To create curves, GOs are grouped nationally by credit rating and the availability of bond insurance. State-specific curves are available. Revenue bonds are classified by the type of project, including roads, bridges, schools, hospitals, and power plants.

This type of relative-value analysis only goes so far because it's based on tax-free yields. Tax rates differ from state to state and from investor to investor, so creating taxable-equivalent yield curves comparable to those for governments and corporate debt becomes impossible.

Because of this limitation, investors track yields on municipal securities as a percentage of Treasury yields, as shown in Exhibit 6.3. When they surpass 100 percent, investors are better off owning state and local debt regardless of tax benefits. They are usually lower than the 100 percent threshold, which means municipals would be more rewarding only because of their tax-exempt status.

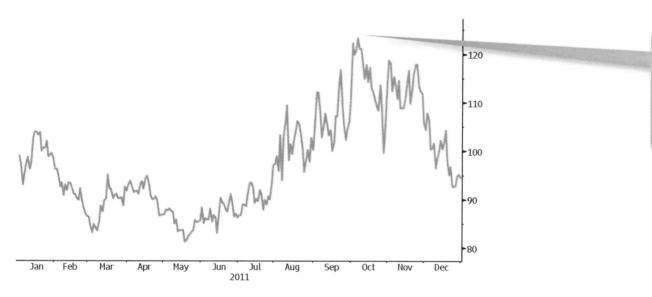

Yields on top-rated municipal debt were as much as 123 percent of Treasury yields during 2011. This means the state and local government bonds were cheaper even without tax benefits.

Exhibit 6.3: AAA Municipal Bond Yield as Percentage of 10-Year Treasury Yield

Mortgage-Backed Securities

Many home buyers across the United States suffered for years from the aftereffects of a housing market bubble that burst in 2007. The same can be said for the investors who ended up owning their mortgages.

The investors didn't purchase the home loans. Instead, they bought securities that were backed by groups of mortgages, known as pools. These bonds entitled the holders to receive a portion of the principal and interest payments on the loans as they were made.

When the bubble ended, many homeowners were unable to keep up with those payments. Others decided not to make them because they owed more than their houses were worth. Either way, many of the mortgage-backed securities became worthless, and others lost much of their value. Investors were hurt by the ripple effect.

The market where these losses occurred was largely a creation of the government even before the housing boom ended. After the collapse, its role became even bigger. It's possible to view MBS as another method of lending money to the government.

Why would investors do that now, especially after the losses that many of them suffered? They're in a position to earn higher returns from these securities than from Treasuries, as they did when home buying was booming. The housing market's collapse reduced the risks associated with the bonds.

That's getting ahead of ourselves. Before we go to the three Rs, we need to understand more about the basics. MBS are part of a category that's called structured finance or securitized products. Structured investments are created by setting up pools of assets and selling securities that are tied to different portions of the pool.

Asset-backed securities (ABS) are in this category. These bonds are backed by loans other than mortgages, including credit card balances, home equity, auto loans, and manufactured housing loans. The debt is repackaged and sold the same way as MBS. The biggest difference is that the government doesn't play a direct role in this market. Private companies do all the work.

In the mortgage market, Fannie Mae and Freddie Mac buy loans from banks and other lenders and move them into trusts, which create the pools. The agencies started out as government-sponsored enterprises (GSEs), or private companies created by Congress, to expand the mortgage market and were taken over in 2008 after home prices plunged.

The Government National Mortgage Association (GNMA or Ginnie Mae) guarantees payments on securities sold by trusts that consist of government-insured loans. Financial companies buy the loans and create the trusts because Ginnie Mae doesn't purchase mortgages as Fannie Mae and Freddie Mac do.

The trusts are known as real estate mortgage investment conduits (REMICs). They can sell bonds known as passthrough securities, which entitle investors to some of the interest and principal from the pooled mortgages. They can sell collateralized mortgage obligations (CMOs), which represent the right to payments on a specified portion of the pool.

CMO sales consist of multiple classes, or tranches, of securities. By design, some tranches suffer losses on mortgages and reach maturity sooner than others. This means the bonds are supposed to have varying degrees of risk even though it didn't work out that way when the housing market collapsed.

Loans that don't qualify for government guarantees can serve as collateral for private-label securities, another type of mortgage-backed bond. They include jumbo loans, which exceed buying limits set by Fannie Mae and Freddie Mac. Mortgage strips are created by splitting up interest and principal payments on home loans into separate securities.

For each of these types of securities, the primary market begins with the making and buying of home loans and the creation of pools. Prices are posted as a benchmark for possible sales in the next three months. These to be announced (TBA) prices are based on three criteria: the inclusion of 30-year or 15-year mortgages in the pool, the annual interest rate built into the bonds, and the agency standing behind them.

DEFINITION:
Structured finance

Structured finance is a method of transforming mortgages and other types of loans into securities. The loans are bundled into pools, and bonds backed by the pools are sold to investors.

DEFINITION:
To be announced

To be announced, or TBA, mortgage-backed securities represent partial ownership of a pool of home loans that's going to be created later.

Secondary trading in mortgage-backed debt takes place over the counter, using electronic networks. Bloomberg BondTrader and Tradeweb are among the online marketplaces. Mortgage-backed securities can be packaged along with commercial real-estate bonds and/or corporate loans into collateralized debt obligations (CDOs), asset-backed securities that are similar to CMOs. The CDO market collapsed in the 2008 financial crisis as the securities lost much of their value.

Quotations

Mortgage-backed bond quotes resemble those for other types of debt even though the securities differ. See Exhibit 6.4 for a quote for a TBA security guaranteed by Ginnie Mae.

GNSF: Symbol for Ginnie Mae I, a guarantee program run by the government agency. Securities sold through Fannie Mae and Freddie Mac have their own symbols as well.

CBBT: Pricing source. This quote is based on prices from firms using Bloomberg BondTrader.

Up arrow: Uptick/downtick arrow, showing the direction of the most recent price change.

103-17+: Latest price as a percentage of face value. MBS quotes are in fractions, like Treasury notes and bonds. The 17+ shows the price is between 103 17/32 percent and 103 18/32 percent of face value.

+10+: Change on the day. The + following the 10 means the change is between 10/32 and 11/32.

103-16+/103-17: Bid and ask prices, presented as percentages. There are no volume totals to go along with the prices because trading takes place over the counter.

At 10:09: Time of the latest price.

Op 103-13, Hi 103-20+, Lo 103-08+: Opening, high, and low prices for the current day's trading.

Prev 103-07: Closing price on the previous trading day.

Two pieces of data excluded from the quote are important: the delivery month, October, and the security's interest rate, 3.5 percent. Each month and rate has a price.

Three Rs

The value of mortgage-backed debt is defined by the securities in the pool of mortgages backing them and the loans included in the pool. Some of the loans are paid off early. Others have to be written off because the borrower can't keep up the payments.

All this detail complicates the process of determining which bonds are cheap, expensive, or fairly valued. We'll run across some unique data used in calculating returns, and we'll encounter some risks that are equally distinctive. We'll learn how all this affects relative-value comparisons.

Returns

The Ginnie Mae security in our quote had a 3.5 percent interest rate. The percentage is set below the rates on mortgages that make up the pool, as the gap

> **KEY POINT:**
> Returns on MBS reflect the performance of the pooled loans. Although CMOs are designed to safeguard some investors at the expense of others, everyone can be hurt if enough mortgages go bad.

▲
▼ GNSF CBBT ↑ 103−17+ + 10+   103-16+/103-17
At 10:09 Op 103-13   Hi 103-20+   Lo 103-08+   Prev 103-07

Exhibit 6.4: A Ginnie Mae TBA Mortgage-Bond Quote

covers expenses. A schedule is available for paying out interest and principal from the loans to bond investors.

Beyond that, not much about the return on the security is certain. The same can be said about any other mortgage-backed bond, whether it's a straightforward passthrough security or a more complex CMO.

Complications occur because the mortgages underlying the bonds can be repaid in advance. Some families sell their homes to move into another local house or to relocate. Others repay the debt as part of a refinancing, which allows them to take advantage of lower interest rates.

Once the deals are complete, these mortgages effectively come out of the pool. They're joined by loans on property that goes through foreclosure because the owner falls too far behind in making interest and principal payments.

Either way, the returns on MBS suffer. When loans are paid off, investors have to go without the interest they would have received. They may receive the principal amount sooner than they wanted, depending on how interest rates have moved. When loans go bad, investors lose the principal and the interest.

A statistic called the constant prepayment rate tracks the early payoffs. The rate is a percentage of the balance for all the loans in the pools, and it's calculated on an annual basis. If 1 percent of the balance was repaid ahead of time last month, for example, the constant rate would be 12 percent. Loan defaults have a similar piece of data known as the constant default rate (CDR).

Estimating returns on MBS would require study of two other statistics, linked to the mortgage pool. The weighted average coupon (WAC) is based on rates and balances for all the loans. The weighted average maturity (WAM) is a period of years that reflects the balances and the maturity dates.

Risks

Constant prepayment rates are constant because they are shown as annual percentages. Mortgage holders may repay loans more quickly or more slowly in the future than they have in the past. The pace of a pool's projected payoffs is known as the prepayment speed.

Changes in speed present risks either way. Prepayment risk covers the possibility of a pickup. If the speed increases, then the investor loses a greater amount of interest and gets back a higher percentage of principal.

DEFINITION:
Prepayment

Prepayment is the payoff of home loans before maturity, which reduces the size of a mortgage pool.

Lower interest rates can cause acceleration by encouraging homeowners to refinance. When that's the case, prepayment risk is tied to reinvestment risk. Investors would not only receive money earlier than they probably wanted, but also be unable to earn as much as they did previously unless they purchased riskier securities.

There's also extension risk, the opposite of prepayment risk. When rates rise, mortgages in the pool stay outstanding for longer periods because refinancing doesn't make sense for most homeowners. MBS owners are stuck with relatively low rates and have to wait for an extended period to receive their money.

More general risks come into play as the past few years have illustrated. Mortgage-backed investors bear market risk related to housing as well as the securities. They take on liquidity risk that's linked to the number and variety of available securities. They also face the risk that a faltering economy may cost homeowners their jobs, leaving them unable to make mortgage payments. Interest rate risk and inflation risk are present as well.

Relative Value

The to be announced pools where we found our Ginnie Mae quote break down MBS by loan types, interest payments, and issue dates. Some pools are for 30-year fixed-rate mortgages, the traditional type of loan for U.S. home buyers. Others are limited to 15-year loans. Still others are designed for different types of adjustable-rate mortgages (ARMs), whose interest payments are tied to a benchmark market rate.

These breakdowns provide a starting point for determining which MBS are cheap, expensive, or fairly priced. There's plenty more where that came from when you add in REMICs, passthroughs, CMO tranches, private-label securities, and other variations on mortgage-backed debt.

Comparing the yields on MBS and Treasuries may provide insight into relative value. The spreads signal how much more investors are likely to earn for assuming those risks cited earlier. We'll go beyond the scope of this book if we proceed much further. MBS are harder to analyze than government and corporate debt, even for professional investors.

> **KEY POINT:**
>
> **Lower interest rates cause mortgages to be paid off faster as homeowners refinance. The increase in prepayment speed limits potential gains for mortgage-bond investors as rates decline.**

CHAPTER 7

Companies Revisited

When companies report on the state of their finances, they make a clear distinction between equity and debt. This isn't as easy to do when looking at variations on their stock and bonds. The three types of securities we'll consider in this chapter, preferred stock, convertible securities, and bank loans, don't fit neatly into either category.

Though companies can count preferred stock as equity, the dividends they pay on the securities are more in line with bond interest than common-stock payouts. Convertible securities start out as bonds or preferred and end up as common equity, assuming the company's shares perform according to plan. Leveraged loans, or bank loans made to companies with high debt loads, can turn into equity if the borrower goes bust.

For bond investors, preferred stock can be appealing because of its dividends. Convertible securities offer the opportunity for returns that go beyond interest and principal payments or preferred dividends. Bank loans

have floating rates as a rule, so investors aren't locked into fixed payments as they are with most bonds.

Stock investors can reduce market risk by owning preferred or convertible securities thanks to their payouts. They would have a higher standing in a bankruptcy, which matters because companies often have nothing left for common shareholders by the time they reorganize. Investing in leveraged loans would put them further up the legal ladder.

To gain a better understanding of all this, let's consider each of their securities individually, beginning with preferred stock.

Preferred Stock

U.S. banks raised hundreds of billions of dollars in 2008 and 2009 to recover from financial damage caused by bad loans and investments. The funding had to be in the form of equity, rather than debt, to meet capital requirements set by the industry's regulators.

> **KEY POINT:**
>
> While preferred stock can be convertible into common stock, not all convertible securities are preferred. Bonds can also provide holders with the right to swap their securities for common.

Some banks sold common stock to increase their capital. Citigroup Inc., the owner of Citibank, was among them. Bank of America Corp., JPMorgan Chase & Co., Wells Fargo & Co., and other banks took a different route. They sold preferred stock, another form of equity that counted toward their capital requirements.

Investors might have preferred these kinds of securities because they paid higher dividends than common stock as a rule. Bank of America, for example, sold preferred stock in January 2008 with an 8.2 percent annual dividend rate. The payout was about two percentage points higher than the common stock's dividend yield at the time.

The stock's preferred status reflects the safety of the dividend. Companies often can't stop payouts as they can with common stock. Though they may be able to defer one or more preferred dividends, they have to catch up before handing out any money to common stockholders.

There's another reason for investors to prefer this stock: They have a higher legal standing than holders of common stock when a company goes into bankruptcy. Owners of preferred stock may end up with something in a reorganization even if common-stock investors get nothing.

Many companies have a reason to prefer bonds and bank loans to raise money. They can deduct interest payments on income tax returns as a business expense. Preferred dividends normally aren't entitled to this deduction because they have to be paid from after-tax profits. As a result, they cost more than interest paid at the same rate or lower rates.

To get around the limitation on deductions, companies can create trusts that sell preferred stock and lend them the money raised from the sale. Interest payments on the loan cover dividend payments on the shares, known as trust preferred. The company can then take the interest deduction.

Financial companies, especially banks, and utilities dominate the preferred stock market. Companies in these industries need to raise large amounts of money to operate and to keep regulators happy. The requirements in other industries aren't as severe.

Preferred stock is initially sold through underwriters like common shares. The price setting process differs because preferred has a par value that's similar to the face value for bonds. The securities firms handling the sale work with the seller to set the dividend rate, meaning the price paid annually for the use of the money.

Once the sale is completed, preferred stock can trade on exchanges or over the counter. Companies that are listed on the NYSE and NASDAQ will typically arrange to have their preferreds listed there as well.

Quotations

Preferred stock quotes are basically the same as corporate bond quotes. Exhibit 7.1 shows a JPMorgan Chase preferred issue, originally sold in August 2008, as an example.

JPM 8⅝% J $ ↓ **27.110** -.390 N N27.110/27.180N   1x2
At 14:50 Vol 126,376 Op 27.450 N Hi 27.450 N Lo 27.050 N Prev 27.500

Exhibit 7.1: A JPMorgan Chase Preferred-Stock Quote

Rather than reviewing all the data in detail, let's look at a few key points:

8 5/8%: Annual dividend rate for the preferred, which is similar to the coupon rate on a bond. Owners of JPMorgan's preferred will receive payouts amounting to 8 5/8 percent of the face value of their securities.

J: Series of the preferred, as designated by JPMorgan. A single letter is usually enough to distinguish these securities from other JPMorgan preferred. If not, then companies are free to use two letters.

27.110: Market price in dollars, comparable to the $25 par amount. The shares are trading at a premium, which means their dividend yield will be less than the 8 5/8 percent rate.

Three Rs

Companies that buy preferred stock receive tax benefits, as individual investors do when they purchase municipal bonds. They have to be taken into account when calculating returns on the securities. They increase demand for the shares, which helps explain why companies sell them even though they can be a costly way to raise funds.

The dividend payments and tax savings provide a basis for judging which preferred shares are cheap, expensive, or fairly priced and for comparing them with other assets. Their risks are similar to those for other corporate securities.

Returns

Price changes and dividend payments largely account for returns on preferred stock as they do with common shares. The similarity only goes so far as prices have less room to move and dividends play a bigger role.

Preferred stock has a par value that's more than a nominal amount. It's similar to the face value of notes and bonds. The JPMorgan Chase stock is valued at $25 each, a price tag within the reach of individual investors. The stock represents partial ownership—1/400th of a share, to be precise—of preferred with a $10,000 par value.

The stock's price reflects the par value and the dividend yield that investors demand to own the stock. The $27.11 price in our quote amounts to a dividend yield of about 7.95 percent, based on the $25 value.

Dividends on preferred stock are usually higher than those on common stock, which means they account for

> **KEY POINT:**
> Preferred stock is quoted in dollars and cents, not as a percentage of par value. Even so, the face amount is a reference point for the price, as 100 is for bonds.

more of the return. The yield on JPMorgan Chase's security was more than triple the dividend yield on the bank's common at the time of the quote. Exhibit 7.2 tracks the yield gap between the two securities.

On the other hand, preferred dividends are less of a sure thing than interest on bonds. As noted earlier, companies can delay payouts on some securities. They are called cumulative preferred because payouts accumulate and must be made in full before the company pays common stock dividends. Preferred can be non-cumulative, and the JPMorgan Chase security is an example.

We need to revisit one more element of returns: the tax break available to companies that purchase them. This provision, called the dividends received deduction, exempts U.S. companies from paying taxes on 70 percent of the dividend payments they receive.

The deduction, also available on common stock, minimizes the risk of triple taxation on the payouts. Unless a company sells trust preferred, only after-tax funds can be used for dividends. The company receiving the funds and its shareholders would also have to pay income taxes if not for the regulation.

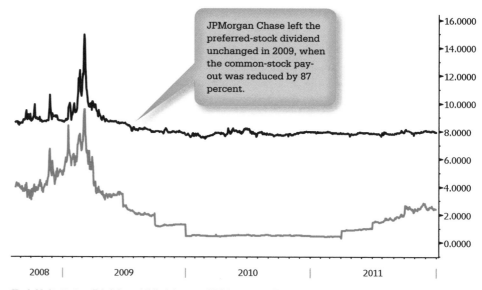

Exhibit 7.2: Dividend Yields on JPMorgan Chase Preferred and Common Stock

Risks

Preferred stock carries the same business risk, event risk, and industry risk as other corporate securities. The degree of risk that investors have to assume falls somewhere between those associated with bills, notes, and bonds and common stock.

Companies that run into financial setbacks can put off dividends on cumulative preferred and skip payouts entirely on non-cumulative stock. This isn't an option with debt payments, which must be made according to schedule for companies to avoid bankruptcy filings or reorganizations.

Inflation risk, interest rate risk, and reinvestment risk are present as they are with companies' debt. The pace of price increases and rate changes affect the value of preferred dividends. If rates fall, investors may have to settle for less income when they reinvest payouts.

Call risk is another concern for preferred stock investors because the stock can be callable, like bonds. Falling interest rates or a pickup in business may lead companies to exercise the option and refinance at a lower cost.

Relative Value

Dividend yields are as fundamental a gauge of relative value for preferred stock as yields are for notes and bonds. Historical yields on a specific security provide perspective on whether it's worth buying, selling, or holding. Yield gaps between a company's preferred issues, or between its preferred and common stock, show how much more investors will earn by choosing one security over another. Comparing the yields on stock sold by different companies does the same.

Earnings, cash flow, debt levels, and other indicators can add meaning to these comparisons. If a company is in a better financial position to pay preferred dividends, then the stock price ought to rise, causing the dividend yield to drop. The opposite can happen.

Convertible Securities

Bank of America made more than one preferred-stock sale in response to the financial crisis. So did Citigroup, which didn't stop with selling common stock. Both banks sold preferred shares that the owner could convert into common shares.

By providing this option, the banks were able to raise money at a lower cost than they might have otherwise. Bank of America's convertible preferred carried a 7.25 percent dividend, and Citigroup's was 6.5 percent. Payouts on other preferred issues that couldn't be swapped for common were at least 8 percent.

Convertible bonds provide similar savings in interest expense by comparison with plain vanilla debt, which can't be exchanged. The lower cost reflects the value that investors put on the option to convert, which rises along with the company's common-stock price.

A price is built into this option when the securities are first sold. It's called the conversion price, and it's

STEP-BY-STEP: VALUING CONVERTIBLES

1. Assume the security has a face value of $1,000 and is convertible at $50 a common share, leading to a conversion ratio of 20.
2. When the common exceeds $50, multiply the market price by the ratio to determine the convertible's value. At a $60 stock price, the security is worth about $1,200.
3. When the common is less than $50, the interest or dividend rate would dictate value. At $40, the convertible would trade for more than the $800 price implied by the conversion ratio.

based on the stock's market price. If a company's stock trades at $40, the conversion might be set at a 25 percent premium, or $50 a share.

The price results in a conversion ratio, or the number of shares that an investor would receive in an exchange. In our example, assume the security has a $1,000 face value. Divide the $50 price into that amount, and the result shows an investor would receive 20 shares of common stock for each convertible security.

Convertible bonds have a maturity date, which means any exchange has to be completed before then. Companies can establish similar limits on preferred securities by giving themselves the right to buy back the stock or requiring their conversion after a specified period.

If the stock rises above the conversion price, then the security's value will be tied to the number of shares that a holder would receive rather than the security's interest or dividend payments.

If the stock doesn't surpass the conversion price, the interest or dividend rate would largely determine the value of the security. The option to convert is worth something as well. The value depends on the gap between the conversion price and the stock price and the amount of time left for the differential to close.

Convertible securities are sold by a broader range of companies than preferred stock. Any company whose common stock has been a top performer might raise money this way because the funds may not have to be repaid. Instead, the convertible debt or preferred

may be exchanged for common stock, enabling the company to increase its equity financing.

Sales are made in the primary market through underwriters as they are for other types of securities. Convertible debt is likely to trade over the counter after the initial sale, and convertible preferred may be listed on an exchange along with the seller's common shares.

Quotations

Convertible bonds and preferred stock are quoted like their peers that aren't convertible. Some differences are apparent when taking a closer look. Exhibit 7.3 shows an Intel Corp. convertible bond quote as an example.

3 1/4: Annual interest rate. For convertible preferred, this would be the dividend rate. Either way, the rate is lower than it would be for a security that isn't convertible. The gap represents what investors are giving up for the right to receive common stock in the future.

117.900: Price as a percentage of face value or par value for convertible preferred. Because the price is more than 100, the yield will be less than 3 1/4 percent.

YLD 2.367: Yield at the current market price. The quote might have noted the yield spread between the Intel bond and a comparable Treasury security: −117bp vs T4 3/8 05/41. It's negative because Intel

INTC3 ¼ 08/39 $ ↓ 117.900 −.975
At 14:16 Vol 3,018 Op 118.500 Hi 118.500 Lo 117.900 YLD 2.367 TRAC

Exhibit 7.3: An Intel Convertible-Bond Quote

can borrow more cheaply than the U.S. government. That's only possible because the notes, unlike Treasuries, can be exchanged for common stock.

Three Rs

Price changes on convertible securities can occur as interest rates rise or fall, affecting the value of their payouts. The market price of the company's common stock may fluctuate, causing the gap between the market price and the conversion price to change.

If the common stock price rises high enough, the returns on the convertible debt or preferred may depend largely on changes in the stock price. Otherwise, they are more closely linked to the interest or dividends that are paid.

Investors in convertibles bear the same risks as common stockholders though they usually receive higher payouts from the company in return for assuming them.

Returns

Convertible securities produce returns through price changes and payouts, either as bond interest or preferred stock dividends. Though we have seen these combinations before, they have a different look this time because

the change in price may reflect the performance of the common stock rather than the convertible.

Let's take the Intel convertibles as an example. The bonds have a face value of $1,000 and can be swapped for common stock at $22.448 a share, which means 44.55 is the conversion ratio. If the stock trades at $30, then multiplying by 44.55 will result in a price of $1,336.50 for each bond. A quote at that price would read 133.65 because it's equivalent to 133.65 percent of par.

When the common stock price is lower than the conversion price, the differential won't dictate the returns on convertible securities as noted earlier. For bonds, the face value and interest payments are what count the most. For preferred stock, the par value and dividends play the same role.

The option to convert the bonds or preferred is worth something as well even if it doesn't make sense to exercise right away. The value of this feature declines as the time to conversion gets closer, which works against investors if the common stock doesn't rise enough to justify a conversion.

Risks

Business risk, event risk, and industry risk are as significant for investors in convertible securities as they are for owners of other debt and preferred stock.

> **KEY POINT:**
>
> **The right to convert bonds and preferred stock always has some value. The amount of value determines whether investors are better off owning convertibles or securities that don't have this feature.**

The conversion feature intensifies the effect of these risks. If they prevent the common stock from rising above the conversion price, the investor will get nothing for accepting the low interest or dividend payments on the convertible.

Risks that go along with owning debt securities are present. Interest rate risk, inflation risk, and reinvestment risk arise with bond interest and preferred-stock dividends. Call risk is another concern for investors, as convertible securities can also be callable.

Relative Value

Two basic approaches are used to decide whether a convertible security is cheap, expensive, or fairly priced. The first is to compare the yield on the bond or preferred stock to yields on similar securities. The second is to compare the value of the common stock that's available in a conversion and the option to convert with the stock's market value.

Starting with the yield is more appropriate for relative-value analysis when the security's conversion price is higher than the common stock price. That's because there's less of a price differential between convertibles and other bonds or preferred shares that can't be turned into common. Exhibit 7.4 tracks the difference in yield between our Intel convertible and Treasuries.

The option to convert still has a value, which we'll see when we examine options. Comparisons with other securities have to account for the value. Otherwise, the results may be misleading.

Price is more revealing than yield when the common stock exceeds the conversion price. Relative value for convertibles hinges on price differences between the securities and the underlying stock.

The Intel convertible should trade at 133.65 when the stock is at $30 as noted earlier. If the bond is quoted at 130, then it will be a cheaper way to buy a stake in the company. If the quote is 135, then the common stock will be a better value.

It's possible to bet on changes in the relative price of convertibles and common shares by purchasing one security and selling the other short at the same time. This strategy, known as convertible arbitrage, is designed to profit from any price gaps between markets. Some hedge funds focus on this kind of trading as we'll find out later.

Bank Loans

Think about the reference to leveraged loans at the beginning of this chapter. This phrase seems redundant somehow. Companies that borrow money are said to have financial leverage. They become leveraged by taking out loans. This suggests every bank loan might be leveraged by definition.

In practice, it doesn't work that way. Companies that have borrowed relatively large amounts of money are said to be leveraged. They have to pay a high price, in the form of an interest rate, to obtain any more funds. If they're able to persuade lenders to make the money available, the result will be a leveraged loan.

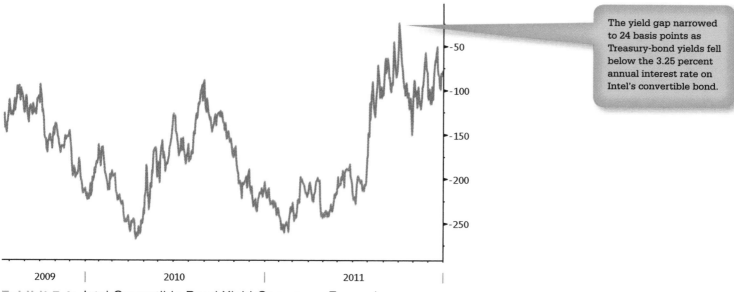

The yield gap narrowed to 24 basis points as Treasury-bond yields fell below the 3.25 percent annual interest rate on Intel's convertible bond.

Exhibit 7.4: Intel Convertible-Bond Yield Gap versus Treasuries

This type of loan dates back to the 1980s, when leveraged buyouts (LBOs) emerged as a way to finance takeovers of multibillion-dollar companies. Buyouts allow financiers to acquire companies mainly with borrowed money, which they obtain by pledging their targets' assets as collateral.

These days, the loans are made to heavily indebted companies, not just because of buyouts. They typically carry floating rates that are based on the London Interbank Offered Rate (Libor). Loans with rates set at least 150 basis points, or 1.5 percentage points, more than Libor fit into the category.

Leveraged loans dominate the bank-loan market. They are a banking equivalent of high-yield bonds, and their performance has been comparable to non-investment grade debt. Exhibit 7.5 shows the relationship.

Leveraged loans are syndicated, which means responsibility for providing the money is shared by a group of banks. Lending to investment-grade companies can be done the same way. Each syndicate has an arranger, who plays much the same role as an underwriter in a sale of securities. The biggest difference is that arrangers don't always guarantee the loan will be made, as underwriters would.

DEFINITION:
Syndicated

Syndicated loans are made through a group of banks, rather than a single lender. One member of the group arranges the loan.

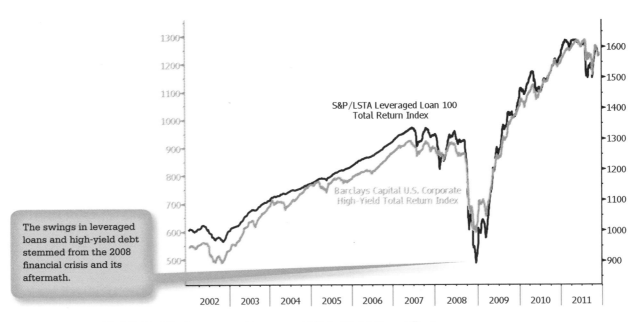

> The swings in leveraged loans and high-yield debt stemmed from the 2008 financial crisis and its aftermath.

Exhibit 7.5: Leveraged Loan and High-Yield Bond Performance

The most popular forms of syndicated lending include term loans, which are made for a specified number of years and must be repaid when they mature. Credit facilities provide companies with more flexible ways to borrow money, such as revolving loans, a corporate equivalent of a credit card. Companies can borrow when funds are needed, and repay them when they aren't, for as long as the revolving credit stays available. Syndicates often provide multiple types of financing in a single agreement.

First-lien loans are a secured form of debt whose holders have first priority on a borrower's assets in bankruptcy. These loans are similar to first mortgages on commercial buildings or homes. Second-lien loans resemble second mortgages because the lenders have a lower standing than the first-lien lenders if the company goes bust.

Once a leveraged loan has been signed, sealed, and delivered, members of the syndicate can sell their portion in a secondary market. These sales take place over the counter in a marketplace dominated by banks, fund managers, and other institutional investors.

Leveraged loans can be repackaged into collateralized loan obligations (CLOs), just as home loans can be transformed into collateralized mortgage obligations (CMOs). CLO sales are done in much the same way as CMOs, with multiple tranches of securities. The owners of these bonds share in payments on the loans and have rights to the collateral backing them.

Quotations

Hertz Global Holdings Inc. (Hertz), a car rental company, borrowed $1.6 billion in March 2011 to refinance debt. Lenders provided most of the funds through a $1.4 billion term loan. Exhibit 7.6 shows a quote for that loan.

HTZ: Symbol for Hertz's debt. The symbol for this loan on the Bloomberg terminal is **HTZ TL 1L**, with TL signifying a term loan and 1L designating a first-lien loan.

0: Placeholder for the interest rate. Hertz pays 275 basis points more than three-month Libor. The period corresponds to the schedule for interest payments on the loan.

3/11/18: Maturity date, March 11, 2018. The term loan and the letter of credit mature in seven years.

$: Dollars, the currency that Hertz borrowed.

Up arrow: Uptick/downtick arrow, showing the direction of the most recent price change.

99.125: Price, stated as a percentage of par value.

+.125: Change on the day.

98.625/99.625: Bid and ask prices.

At 11:00: Time of the latest price quote.

Op 99.000, Hi 99.125, Lo 99.000: Opening, high, and low prices for the current day's trading.

Prev 99.000: Previous day's closing price.

BVAL: Bloomberg Valuation, the pricing source. Other prices are available from the Loan Syndication and Trading Association, a trade group whose market index appeared in Exhibit 7.5, and from banks and brokers.

Three Rs

Leveraged loans can be described as high-yield, floating-rate debt. High yield means the interest payments account for a larger part of returns than they do

```
HTZ  0 03/11/18 $ ↑ 99.125 +.125  98.625/99.625
     At 11:00  Op 99.000  Hi 99.125  Lo 99.000  Prev 99.000  BVAL
```
Exhibit 7.6: A Hertz Leveraged-Loan Quote

for investment-grade loans, as is the case for bonds. The floating rate ensures the payments will fluctuate along with the level of interest rates, and the returns will swing along with them.

Lenders take on the risks associated with companies and debt, and they are magnified because the borrower's financial position is comparatively weak. Yields on the loans provide a basis for relative-value analysis.

Returns

The familiar combination of price changes and interest payments accounts for the returns on leveraged loans. Prices tend to increase as a borrower's business and financial performance improves, and vice versa. Interest rises and falls along with Libor, based on the spread associated with the loan.

When Hertz had to make the first payment on its loan in June 2011, the three-month dollar Libor was about 0.25 percent, or 25 basis points. Add the 275 basis point spread, and Hertz paid interest at a 3 percent annual rate. When the second payment was due, Libor was near 0.35 percent. This raised the floating rate to an annualized 3.1 percent.

Rising interest rates can increase demand for leveraged loans because of their floating payments. Fixed rate securities and loans tend to lose value when rates move higher, as the only way to keep their yields in line with market rates is to reduce the price.

> **KEY POINT:**
>
> Floating rates on leveraged loans are designed to adjust for swings in market interest rates, rather than changes in a company's performance.

Risks

The relationship between interest rates and loan demand isn't constant. If Libor and other benchmark rates surge, then the value of leveraged loans will likely drop. Higher rates may increase the risk that borrowers will fail to keep up the payments and hurt their business.

Credit risk is the issue in the first scenario. As the risk grows, loan prices fall because the interest payment formula may no longer provide enough compensation to satisfy lenders. A cut to Hertz's credit ratings may justify an interest rate of Libor plus 325 basis points for its loan, rather than Libor plus 275, for example. Because the formula won't change, the price does.

Default risk follows from credit risk, and it's another concern for leveraged loan investors. Interest rate risk, inflation risk, and reinvestment risk must be examined even though the floating rate minimizes them to a degree.

Higher interest rates may weigh on Hertz because of their effect on economic growth. Fewer people may be able or willing to travel, hurting demand for rental cars. This is an economic risk and a business risk as Hertz is the kind of company whose results are especially sensitive to the economy's performance.

Industry risk and event risk are part of the mix as well. Too much competition among rental car companies may hamper Hertz's ability to draw customers.

Competitors may be reducing rental rates to win more business, hurting the company's profits and cash flow. Changes in tax laws, management, agreements with car companies, and other events may lead to business setbacks.

Relative Value

Yields provide a way to determine whether leveraged loans are cheap, expensive, or fairly priced, as they do for bonds. Formulas for interest payments, credit ratings, and other criteria add depth to relative-value analysis.

Comparisons between loan yields are easy enough because floating rates are the norm. The process gets more complicated when comparing the loans with high-yield bonds, another mainstay of financing for less creditworthy companies. The bonds typically have fixed rates, so their yields are more certain as long as the company can make the payments.

To overcome this hurdle, investors can calculate a fixed-rate equivalent yield for the loans. Data compiled by Bloomberg shows, for example, that a 3.75 percent yield on Hertz's loan equals about 4.5 percent at a fixed rate. High-yield debt maturing at about the same time might yield 6.75 percent.

The lower yield reflects the loan's safety, another consideration in relative-value analysis. The leveraged loan is secured. If Hertz doesn't pay the interest and repay the principal when it's due, lenders have a legal right to seize the collateral. The high-yield bonds, by contrast, are unsecured.

Interest formulas and credit ratings, taken together, can show whether the yield is appropriate. Comparing the formulas will show who's paying less or more to borrow. Ratings from S&P, Moody's, and other services, along with investors' own credit analysis, shed light on whether the loans' interest payments and yields are reasonable.

CHAPTER 8

Hard Assets Revisited

David Einhorn, the founder of Greenlight Capital, is a hedge-fund manager who's better known for his pans than his picks. He sold Lehman Brothers Holdings Inc.'s stock short before the securities firm went bankrupt in 2008. He prevailed in a six-year fight against Allied Capital Inc., a small business lender, that he wrote about in the book *Fooling Some of the People All of the Time.* He bet against St. Joe Co., a real estate developer whose biggest shareholder was Bruce Berkowitz's Fairholme Fund, among the best-performing U.S. mutual funds of the 2000s.

Yet Einhorn's track record creates interest in what he's buying, not just what he's selling short. In the third quarter of 2011, he bet gold mining stocks would do better than gold bullion, which he had previously bought on behalf of a publicly traded company he chairs.

On a conference call, Einhorn disclosed he sold some of the metal and put the money into a gold mining stock fund. The fund tracks the performance of the NYSE Arca Gold Miners Index, which had climbed with the price of gold for more than two years before falling off the pace in the first half of 2011. Exhibit 8.1 illustrates the index's relative performance.

This kind of variation on the theme of hard assets isn't unique to Einhorn. Some investors own mining stocks as well as gold and other metals, or as a substitute for them. Others make similar choices with energy companies and the commodities that they provide or with agricultural stocks and farm products.

Bond markets offer investment opportunities with a hard asset twist. Notes and bonds sold by commodity producers are among them, along with government securities sold by Australia, Canada, South Africa, and other countries whose economies are most closely tied to commodities.

This approach can apply to real estate investing. Higher property prices can have a spillover effect on shares of developers and construction companies.

KEY POINT:

Investing in commodity producers and real estate companies is one alternative to buying hard assets. Another is investing in locations dependent on commodities or real estate.

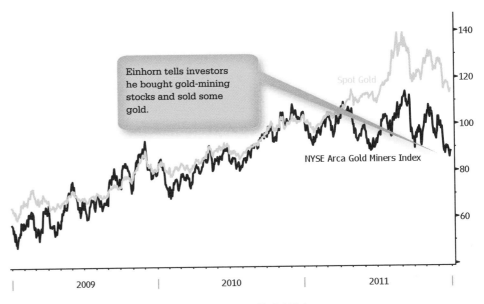

Exhibit 8.1: Gold-Mining Stocks versus Gold Price

Increased demand for land can lift the shares of companies that own thousands of acres or more. The same can be said for their bonds, whose value may increase as the companies' prosperity reduces their credit risk.

Companies known as passthrough entities are another type of investment linked to hard assets. They pass through earnings to investors, just as mortgage passthroughs entitle holders to a piece of principal and interest payments on the mortgages that back them.

These entities are master limited partnerships, which focus on commodity-related businesses, and real estate investment trusts, which own property. Both are exempted from corporate income taxes as long as they meet criteria set by the U.S. government. Let's take a closer look at each.

Master Limited Partnerships

Kinder Morgan Inc. put itself in position to control the largest network of U.S. energy pipelines in October

> **DEFINITION:**
> **Passthrough entities**
>
> These entities pass through earnings to investors, rather than paying income taxes on the profits. The tax exemption lets them pay higher dividends than corporations.

2011, when the company agreed to buy El Paso Corp. for $21.1 billion. The deal brought together the two companies along with two publicly traded units that managed the bulk of their assets.

Kinder Morgan Energy Partners LP owned or operated about 28,000 miles of pipelines, as well as 180 terminals for storing oil products and chemicals. El Paso Pipeline Partners LP had a more extensive pipeline network, covering 43,000 miles, along with a liquefied natural gas terminal.

Both units had Partners in their names, followed by the LP identifier, for a reason. They were master limited partnerships (MLPs), which combine the tax benefits of partnerships with the ease of buying and selling that goes along with exchange-listed securities. MLPs got their start with the federal Tax Reform Act of 1986, which defined the kinds of companies that were eligible and the requirements to qualify.

Most MLPs are in energy-related and commodity-related businesses as Kinder Morgan's and El Paso's partnerships are. Leveraged buyout (LBO) firms, which use funds raised from investors and borrowed money to acquire companies, are among the exceptions. Blackstone Group LP, KKR & Co. LP, and other firms reorganized as MLPs to go public. We'll find out more about their business later.

MLPs have partnership units, rather than common stock. Owners of the securities are defined as unitholders, not shareholders. They are also limited partners, who typically own a 98 percent stake as a group. Management is left to the general partner, which has

the other 2 percent and is paid based on the MLP's performance. Kinder Morgan is a general partner, and El Paso played that role.

Payouts on the units are known as distributions and are made quarterly. They are based on cash flows, rather than net income, and are usually larger than dividends paid on common shares. The checks are bigger because MLPs can pass along earnings without paying corporate income taxes first.

This exemption explains why energy and commodity producers create MLPs in the first place. To keep their status, MLPs have to generate at least 90 percent of taxable income every year from sources specified as qualifying by the Internal Revenue Service (IRS). They can include dividends and interest payments, as well as income from their business.

Some investors stay away from MLPs because of the tax complications. For others, the additional income they provide is more than enough to justify having to do some extra recordkeeping.

MLP units are available through the same primary market as stocks. The partnerships make initial public offerings (IPOs) with the help of underwriters. Once the IPOs are complete, the units are listed on exchanges or are traded in the over-the-counter (OTC) market.

Quotations

MLP units are quoted the same way as common shares, as exchanges provide the same data for them. Enterprise Products Partners LP (Products),

---

KEY POINT:

Most master limited partnerships focus on energy or commodities. Leveraged-buyout firms, which buy companies mainly with borrowed money, are exceptions.

DEFINITION:
Distributions

Distributions by master limited partnerships are comparable to dividend payments by other companies. They are usually larger because MLPs are exempt from corporate income taxes.

EPD US $ ↓ **40.62** -.67 Z N40.59/40.63B   8x1
At 14:30 Vol 443,731 Op 41.28 N Hi 41.40 T Lo 40.50 Z ValTrd 18112594

Exhibit 8.2: Quote for the Enterprise Products MLP

which transports and processes natural gas, is a good example (see Exhibit 8.2).

All the details that we saw for Apple Inc.'s stock are here. The first line has the ticker symbol, exchange code, dollar sign, uptick/downtick arrow, latest price, change on the day, and bid and ask quotes. The second line shows the 24-hour time of the latest trade, the current day volume, the open, high, and low prices, and the stock value traded in thousands of dollars. Both lines have one-letter exchange IDs next to all their prices.

Three Rs

MLPs tend to focus on pipelines, terminals, and other stable segments of energy and commodity production. Surging prices for oil, natural gas, and other products may have little effect on the market value of their units. The tradeoff for investors is that the units generate more income than most common stock thanks to their tax status. Their distributions are largely responsible for returns.

The risks of MLP investing are largely tied to the potential for distributions to decline, rather than rise. Distribution rates represent a basis for comparing partnership units with each other, and with different types of securities, in relative-value analysis.

Returns

Price changes and payouts add up to returns on MLP units as they do for other forms of equity as well as debt. Even so, these two components have characteristics that are unlike what we saw with their counterparts.

MLP units don't necessarily track energy and commodity prices even when the shares of producers do. Enterprise Products, the MLP from our quote, shows the performance gaps that can occur. In 2005, the units fell 7 percent even though natural gas rose 83 percent in New York trading. The reverse was true five years later, as Enterprise Products gained 32 percent in the face of a 21 percent drop in gas prices.

Investors in the units have more of a sure thing in distributions, known legally as quarterly required distributions (QRDs). The amounts are specified in a contract between the general and limited partners that governs the MLP.

They also have more tax issues, which affect after-tax returns on the units. Distributions are taxed differently from dividends or interest payments. Any portion that exceeds taxable income is subtracted from the price you paid for the units. This reduces what's known as their cost basis. If you sell the securities, the lower cost basis may mean a larger gain, and a bigger tax bill to match.

Unit owners have to pay their share of the MLP's annual income tax bill because the exemption only applies to the partnership. MLPs hand out forms, designated as Schedule K-1s by the IRS, which show how much each investor owes.

Risks

The ultimate risk for MLP investors is that a partnership won't make a quarterly required distribution on schedule. This is a form of default risk, as it's similar to a company missing an interest payment or failing to repay principal when it's due on notes or bonds.

Anything that puts the partnership closer to a default constitutes a risk. The business may fail to retain customers, causing revenue to decline. Price cutting by competitors may require the partnership to follow suit, another potential blow to revenue. Takeovers, asset purchases and sales, and natural disasters are among the events that may hurt MLPs and their investors.

Relative Value

Yields tied to payouts are a more useful relative-value indicator for MLP units than for common stock. For one thing, the distributions that determine them are about as certain as interest payments on bonds. For another, MLPs' exemption from income taxes means unitholders will receive more money than owners of common stock get from dividends.

There's one more reason why MLPs are attractive. The yields largely explain why investors buy the securities in the first place even with all their tax complications. The Alerian MLP Index, a benchmark consisting of 50 partnerships, yielded about 6 percent near the end of 2011. That was almost triple the yield on the Standard & Poor's 500 Index and the 10-year Treasury note. Exhibit 8.3 illustrates the comparison.

This kind of comparison provides insight into whether MLPs are cheap, expensive, or fairly valued. Historical yield spreads between their units and stocks, Treasury securities, or other investments provide more perspective.

Then again, the analysis can only go so far because MLPs have tax advantages. Yields are most directly comparable between partnerships, where there isn't a difference in tax treatment to take into account. If Enterprise Products has a 5.4 percent yield and Kinder Morgan Energy Partners yields 5.9 percent, as they did in December 2011, the half-percentage-point gap is meaningful on its own.

Distribution growth is another consideration in relative-value analysis for MLPs. The faster that payouts are rising, the more likely it is that the units' yield will be maintained or increase. Payouts at Enterprise Products, for instance, rose at an annual rate

> **DEFINITION:**
> **Cost basis**
>
> The cost basis of a security is the price used to calculate gains and losses for tax purposes, which can differ from the original purchase price.

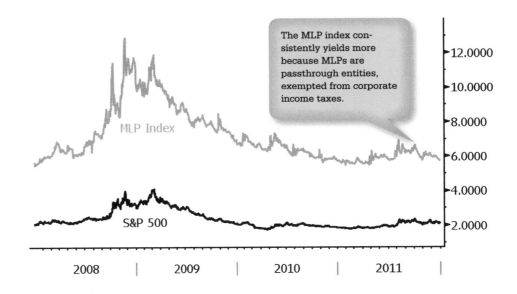

Exhibit 8.3: Alerian MLP Index Dividend Yield versus Standard & Poor's 500 Index Yield

of 6 percent for the five years ended in 2011. The pace of growth at Kinder Morgan's partnership was even faster, 7.2 percent, in the period. Both figures were higher than the distribution yield, a favorable sign for future payouts.

The financial ratios used to evaluate common stocks apply to MLPs. Unit prices relative to earnings, cash flow, and book value are among the indicators used to carry out relative-value analysis.

Real Estate Investment Trusts

Weyerhaeuser Co. can trace its corporate history back to 1900, when a German immigrant named Frederick Weyerhaeuser and 15 partners joined forces to buy 900,000 acres of timberland in the Pacific Northwest.

For the next 110 years, Weyerhaeuser was organized as a corporation. Then the company decided to transform itself into a real estate investment trust (REIT). Once the change was made, Weyerhaeuser no longer had to pay income taxes on its earnings. That made more money available for dividends.

Weyerhaeuser is an exception among REITs because of its status as a forest products company. Most trusts own and manage commercial properties: offices, hotels, apartment buildings, warehouses, and storage facilities. They enable investors to put money into real estate without making the kind of commitment that goes along with buying and running buildings.

REITs as we know them now date back to 1960, when a U.S. law created them. For years, the trusts were largely content to own properties and hire outside managers to run them. They evolved into operators and owners as Weyerhaeuser's conversion to REIT status would suggest.

By law, REITs have to earn at least 95 percent of their income from property and related investments and pay out at least 90 percent of their taxable income to investors. As long as they meet these criteria and others, the profit isn't taxed before being distributed. Only the REIT's investors have to pay income taxes, so there's more money available to hand out to them. The trust's investors are called unitholders, like the limited partners in MLPs.

Dividend and interest income can count toward the 95 percent threshold, and there are REITs that own mortgages and mortgage-backed securities (MBSs). Mortgage REITs invest only in the bonds, and hybrid REITs own property as well as debt securities.

REITs differ from other types of companies because they have their own way of tracking performance. It's a gauge known as funds from operations (FFO) that's calculated by making some adjustments to net income.

FFO adds back depreciation, a charge taken to reflect wear and tear on buildings and equipment, as well as amortization, a similar adjustment for other types of assets. The charges are accounting entries rather than cash payments, and they're at odds with the tendency of real estate values to rise over time.

Any gains or losses from sales of property or investments are subtracted in calculating FFO. Though REITs may sell assets regularly, each deal can only be made once. The proceeds from these sales are unrelated to their daily business, or operations.

REITs make IPOs like other types of companies. Afterward, their units trade on the NYSE, NASDAQ, and competing stock exchanges or in the OTC market.

Since 2001, REITs have been included in Standard & Poor's U.S. stock indexes, such as the S&P 500. S&P made them eligible in recognition of the industry's shift toward running their properties as well as owning them. REITs were omitted before then because they were more like funds than companies.

STEP-BY-STEP: FUNDS FROM OPERATIONS

1. Start with a REIT's net income
2. Add back depreciation and amortization.
3. Subtract net gains or add back net losses from property sales.
4. The result is the REIT's funds from operations.

Quotations

The similarity between REITs and common stock extends to their quotes. Exhibit 8.4 shows a quote for units of Prologis, the world's largest REIT.

There's no difference between this quote and the ones that we saw for Enterprise Products and Apple, aside from the symbol and numbers. The price of the latest trade is shown along with bid, ask, open, high, and low prices, and the exchange code for each. The number of round lots for the bid and ask prices and the numbers of units changing hands are included.

Three Rs

REITs provide the higher dividend yields associated with MLPs without creating the kinds of tax complications presented by the partnerships. These payouts account for much of the return available from REIT units. The rest comes from price changes, as with other types of securities.

Some distinctive risks go with REITs. Market risk goes beyond unit-price changes to include shifts in real estate values, for example. As for relative value, dividend yields are as useful as they are for MLPs. They provide a basis for comparing individual REITs and for assessing trusts as a group relative to other investments.

Returns

REITs are passthrough entities, which is why they're bound by the 90 percent minimum distribution from income each year. They meet this requirement through dividends rather than the distributions that partnerships make. That said, the payouts have the same effect.

When the 90 percent standard is combined with the income tax exemption for REITs, the result is higher dividends than those paid on common stock. The Bloomberg Industries North America REIT Index, for instance, had a dividend yield of about 3.75 percent in December 2011. The yield for this index, composed of about 130 REITs, was about double the corresponding yield for the S&P 500. Exhibit 8.5 shows the differential.

As the comparison suggests, dividends account for a large proportion of REIT returns. Demand for higher yielding investments comes into play because of its effect on prices. As noted earlier, the 10-year Treasury note's yield was about the same as the S&P 500's dividend yield in late 2011. Investors looking for income had an incentive to favor REITs because their payouts were higher.

PLD US $ ↑ **24.48** +1.27 N N24.46/24.48N 17x240
At 16:15 Vol 6,164,970 Op 23.11 T Hi 24.53 N Lo 22.73 N ValTrd 146.605m

Exhibit 8.4: A Quote for the Prologis REIT

REIT prices rise and fall with the trusts' performance. When occupancy rates are increasing and lease or rental rates are climbing, stock prices usually follow suit. When their business isn't faring as well, prices tend to fall. Let's look into the risks more closely.

Risks

Market risk takes on another dimension for REIT investors. The trusts may be hurt by lower real estate values as well as falling stock prices. If the market for offices, stores, and other property held by a REIT worsens, then the value of a trust's assets probably will decline. Any potential gains from selling buildings may be more elusive. The REIT may have a more difficult time finding buyers and making sales, and any properties sold may fetch lower prices than they would command otherwise.

Interest rate risk has another meaning as well. Higher rates may hurt a REIT's sales efforts by increasing the cost of mortgages and may also lead to higher

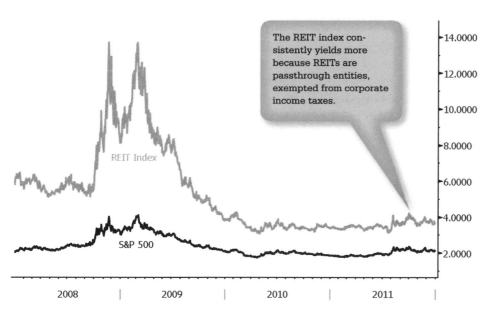

The REIT index consistently yields more because REITs are passthrough entities, exempted from corporate income taxes.

Exhibit 8.5: Bloomberg Industries North American REIT Index Dividend Yield versus Standard & Poor's 500 Index Yield

interest expense on the trust's borrowings. They are less of an issue for investors as payouts are in the form of dividends rather than interest.

Economic risk is much the same for REITs as for other companies. When the economy is expanding, demand increases for offices, stores, hotel rooms, warehouse space, and other business-related property. During recessions, the demand dries up. Apartment buildings are an exception, as shown in the real estate boom and bust during the 2000s. Families are more inclined to buy homes in times of economic growth and stay in rental housing during periods of weakness.

Business risk, industry risk, and event risk are a consideration for REIT investors. When trusts are unable to find or retain tenants, these setbacks may depress the value of their shares. When rivals are luring tenants with more lucrative deals, the holders may be hurt. Takeovers, disasters, and other events may have the same effect.

Relative Value

Investors can determine whether REIT units are cheap, expensive, or fairly priced by analyzing their dividends, which are as useful an indicator as they are for MLPs.

Payouts provide a way to distinguish among REITs that own specific types of property, such as offices or stores. They are a benchmark for comparing REIT categories. Mortgage REITs, which buy securities with borrowed money as well as funds from unitholders, have produced higher dividend yields than trusts that own property.

Dividend yields are a starting point for comparing REIT units with other securities as the earlier references to the S&P 500 and the 10-year Treasury note suggested. The higher the relative payout, the more investors have to gain by taking the risks associated with REITs, and vice versa.

Financial ratios tied to the price of REIT units are helpful. Funds from operations take the place of earnings in the analysis, resulting in price-FFO ratios. The FFO figure may be adjusted for capital spending on property maintenance. Prices relative to cash flow and book value can be used as well.

Debt ratios are one more common denominator for relative-value analysis. Mortgage REITs aren't the only ones who rely on borrowed funds. Trusts turn to banks and bond investors to finance property purchases, and debt loads affect their ability to maintain payouts in the face of business setbacks.

PART II

INDIRECT INVESTING

CHAPTER 9

Overview

Derivatives and funds aren't ordinarily grouped together, yet they both represent indirect ownership of money market securities, notes, bonds, stocks, commodities, real estate, and other assets. Owning a derivative contract differs from having an asset in your possession. Buying shares of a fund isn't the same as having direct control of its holdings.

The connections run deeper. Funds can own derivatives, government and corporate securities, or hard assets. Derivatives are available on shares of funds, especially those that track the Standard & Poor's 500 Index, the Dow Jones Industrial Average, and other benchmarks.

Risk is another common denominator. Derivatives are a way to transfer the risk associated with securities and hard assets. Energy and commodity producers can minimize the risk that price swings will cut into revenue, and investors can protect against losses on their holdings. Investing in funds reduces the risks that go with putting money into individual countries, companies, or hard assets.

At the same time, substantial differences exist. Derivatives last for a specific length of time, as short as a few weeks. Fund shares have no expiration date. Some of the oldest U.S. funds started in the 1920s, and shares sold then may still be around today.

Leverage represents a second point of departure. Buyers of derivatives have to pay a small percentage of a contract's value even though their daily gains and losses are based on the entire amount. Fund investors have to pay full price for shares even though they can borrow part of the money in some cases. Leverage largely depends on the investment strategy followed by the fund and its manager.

Derivatives provide more control of what you own than funds allow. Contracts define the terms and conditions for anyone taking delivery, and they don't usually change over time. Fund assets can differ daily as the manager makes trades. The longer you own the shares, the more extensive the changes are likely to be.

> **DEFINITION:**
> **Leverage**
>
> Financial leverage is the ability to multiply potential gains or losses on an investment. Derivatives provide leverage because the value of contracts is greater than the cost of buying them. Funds have leverage only if the manager borrows money to make investments.

The role of the primary market in derivatives and funds differs as well. Derivative contracts are created and canceled every trading day, and not many are used to raise money as stocks and bonds are. Some funds, by contrast, go public as companies, master limited partnerships (MLPs), and real estate investment trusts (REITs) do.

Then again, the mix of markets is comparable. Derivative exchanges handle trading in standardized contracts though the over-the-counter (OTC) markets have some as well. Customized derivatives are available through OTC markets. Some funds are listed on exchanges, and others change hands through the fund's manager in OTC trading.

Quotations

To understand the price of a derivative, you have to know the contract's terms. Quotes provide some of these key details. Exhibit 9.1 is an example of a futures contract, and Exhibit 9.2 illustrates an option. Both derivatives are based on Eurodollar deposits, and track money market rates.

Expiration: Futures lapse on a set schedule, often monthly or quarterly. Other contracts known as forwards expire after a preset period, such as three months. Time references are in quotes that define the contract's duration.

Total contracts: The number changes daily as new contracts are bought and existing ones are canceled, and the daily swings are usually bigger than you would see with bills, bonds, or stocks. For these reasons, quotes on exchange-traded contracts show what's called open interest, or the number outstanding.

Buy or sell: Options contracts give you the right to do one or the other. Call options represent the right to buy, and put options convey the right to sell. Quotes on any contract define whether it's for buying or selling.

At what price: For many derivatives, the answer is simple: the price paid for the contract. Options add a wrinkle because they lock in the price of a later purchase or sale. That price is inevitably included in option quotes as well.

More details than these are provided in derivative quotes. We'll go through them as we examine each type of contract individually.

Fund quotations depend on who's responsible for the market. In many cases, investors buy and sell shares directly with the fund company after each trading day ends. Exchange codes, trading ranges, or

> **KEY POINT:**
>
> **Derivatives enable investors to transfer risk, especially market risk, to others more willing to bear them. The contract terms define the risk and the length of time it's being shifted.**

```
EDM2 ↓  99.540 --    M 99.540/99.545 M  185x18062
At  9:30 Vol 56,745 Op 99.540  Hi 99.550  Lo 99.535  Prev 99.540
```

Exhibit 9.1: A Eurodollar Futures Quote

`EDZ3P` 98.25 ↓ **.1050 −.0025** M .0900/.1100 M
At 8:24 Op .0900 Hi   Lo .1050a Prev .1075 OpInt 8,439y

Exhibit 9.2: A Eurodollar Options Quote

volume aren't included in their quotes. Other funds are listed on stock exchanges, and their quotes are as detailed as you would see for stocks, MLPs, or REITs.

Three Rs

Returns on derivatives and fund shares depend on the performance of other investments. Most derivative contracts rise and fall along with the value of the security, commodity, or index they represent. The moves may not be identical as timing affects the contracts' price as well.

Fund returns stem from price changes in their investments, along with any interest and dividend payments. Moves may be more limited for funds that track indexes passively than for those whose managers actively make buying and selling decisions, which can enable them to beat the market.

Risks associated with these indirect investments are tied to their underlying assets. For derivatives, the risks are magnified because the amount of money required to buy contracts or sell them short is a small percentage of their value. Funds, on the other hand, tend to be less risky because they own a number of investments.

The underlying assets for derivatives and funds are an essential element in analyzing relative value. The gap between the price of a derivative and the price of a related security, commodity, or index can indicate whether the contract is cheap, expensive, or fairly priced. Financial ratios used to compare funds are based on averages for their investments.

Returns

Derivatives don't pay interest or dividends as a rule, which means price changes are the sole source of returns. The moves are inevitably tied to the price of the underlying asset, and the link grows stronger as the time until contracts expire gets shorter.

Changes in the time to expiration affect returns as the gap between a contract's price and the asset's market price closes on a daily basis. If the derivative price is higher, then the value will decline over time. If it's lower, then the value will increase.

Fund returns are tied to income from their investments, as well as management fees and other expenses. Bond funds receive interest on the securities they own. Stock funds get dividends. Balanced funds, which own debt and equity, receive both. The income helps to cover the fund's costs. Lower expenses mean higher returns. This helps to explain the appeal of index funds, which are generally cheaper.

> **DEFINITION:**
> **Fund returns**
> Passive funds are designed to mirror the returns of an index, and hold some or all of its securities. Active funds aim to beat their benchmark's return and own investments picked by the manager.

> **KEY POINT:**
> Derivatives don't pay interest or dividends even if the underlying asset does. Funds distribute payments on their holdings to shareholders after deducting expenses.

Risks

Before we look at risks that are specific to derivatives and funds, let's review the broader concerns that go with investing. Market risk and liquidity risk are universal as are political risk, economic risk, policy risk, and currency risk. The owners of contracts and fund shares can't escape them.

Interest rate risk and inflation risk affect the value of derivatives and funds tied to bills, notes, and bonds. Funds and their investors bear credit risk, default risk, reinvestment risk, and call risk in connection with debt securities. Business risk, industry risk, and event risk go with contracts and fund shares linked to companies, including stocks and bonds.

With derivatives, we can add two more risks to this lineup. Leverage is a risk because the value of contracts is much higher than the amount of money required to buy them or sell them short would suggest. Counterparty risk is the prospect that the buyer or seller may fail to live up to the contract's obligations. This arises with OTC derivatives as exchanges are the counterparty for their contracts.

Fund shares have risks all their own. Managers can stray from the investment strategy that's laid out for the fund or can make decisions that don't pay off. Even though this isn't a concern for investors in index funds, they face the risk that daily moves in stock prices will fail to mirror the fund's benchmark. This is known as tracking error.

DEFINITION:
Counterparty

Counterparties are the participants in a contract. Buyers and sellers of derivatives are counterparties, and both sides have obligations to meet under the agreements.

Relative Value

There's nothing as straightforward as yields or price-earnings ratios (P/Es) that indicate whether derivatives are cheap, expensive, or fairly priced. For funds, yields and P/Es can be useful with a couple of caveats: They're averages, and the holdings used to calculate them can change at any time.

Relative-value analysis varies for derivatives, based on the type of contract. Futures and options can be compared from one period to another, based on expiration dates. They can be compared with the price of the underlying asset. Option contracts, for example, have a value that goes beyond the asset price. They're worth something even when an investor wouldn't exercise the option as we learned from convertible bonds and preferred stock.

Swaps are exchanges of payments that differ by interest rate, currency, or other criteria. There are two sides to each contract, and it's possible to look at their value from either side. What's cheap for one participant in a swap may be expensive for the other.

Payments in fixed interest rates are a standard feature in some swaps. The rates can be compared with note and bond yields on Treasury securities, as with other forms of debt, as a gauge of value.

Relative-value analysis doesn't stop there. To learn more, let's take a closer look at the three main types of derivatives: futures, options, and swaps. We'll consider forwards in our examination of futures, and learn about warrants as part of our study of options.

CHAPTER 10

Derivatives

Commodities and real estate can be described as real assets, as mentioned earlier. Money market securities, stocks, and bonds are one step removed from reality as their owners have a financial asset rather than something tangible. Even investors in secured bonds don't have a real asset unless a borrower defaults.

Take another step back, and you'll encounter derivatives. These contracts derive their value from a real or financial asset. Derivatives are traded on gold, other commodities, real estate, currencies, interest rates, notes, bonds, stocks, and indexes that track one or more of these assets.

We ran into futures contracts, a type of derivative, when we looked at commodities. The spot price quote that we saw for West Texas Intermediate (WTI) crude oil was based on futures prices, not the other way around. That's because oil futures are among the most actively traded contracts and are far easier to follow

than WTI cargoes. Futures prices are benchmarks for other commodity markets.

It's time to take a closer look at futures as well as forwards, a similar type of contract that's more easily customized. To help illustrate these derivatives and others, we'll bring back a classic comic strip and cartoon character known for his love of hamburgers.

Futures and Forwards

Would you gladly pay someone Tuesday for a hamburger today? If so, you can identify with J. Wellington Wimpy, a friend of Popeye the sailor man. Wimpy hated to spend money, and hamburgers were his favorite meal. He would make this offer at his local diner in an attempt to eat without paying.

Let's turn this around. Would you gladly pay someone today for a hamburger on Tuesday? If you expected the burger to cost more by Tuesday, the answer might be yes. If you could sell the future burger to someone else at the higher price, you might agree.

For those who aren't convinced, let's sweeten the deal. You could lock in today's burger price by paying much less than the full amount. Assuming the diner charged $4, you might only have to set aside a 10-cent deposit. You would save money and earn a profit as long as Tuesday's price was higher than $4. This kind of opportunity is available in futures, because they establish the price of a later purchase or sale. There are futures on the cattle used to make ground beef and the wheat for hamburger rolls, among other commodities. Futures markets began with commodity trading, though contracts to buy and sell stocks, bonds, and money market investments have become far more active.

The hamburger contract in our example wouldn't qualify as a future because there's no exchange that handles the trading and sets the terms. Instead, it resembles a forward contract, or an agreement that's traded over the counter and can be customized. Forward rates are posted in the currency and money markets, and this type of contract can cover other securities and commodities.

Either way, the burger is the underlying asset for the contract. The initial 10-cent cost is called a margin. Futures exchanges determine the amount and require buyers and short sellers to set aside the money in an account. They might have to add funds later, based on daily changes in market value, to maintain the margin. With forwards, there's one payment made

at the time of signing. This means the contracts are riskier than futures as markets move in one direction or the other.

If you paid the 10 cents to avoid the risk of a higher burger price on Tuesday, then you would be hedging. If you did this for a potential profit, you would be speculating. Futures and forward markets exist for hedgers to transfer the risk of price changes to speculators.

The contract would specify the burger you could buy, the time of day you could buy it, and the number you could have at one sitting, among other conditions. Futures exchanges set the terms of their contracts. They often require agreements to be settled through cash payments rather than deliveries of commodities or securities. With forwards, the terms are up to the buyer and seller. This means they can reach an agreement that more closely meets their needs than a futures contract, assuming there's one available for what they're trading.

Futures contracts are easier to trade because they're standardized. Rather than having to take delivery of a commodity or security, the futures buyer can turn around and sell. The reverse is true for sellers, and it's typical for futures to be settled in this way. In other words, futures are more liquid than forwards, which may be an advantage when market prices are moving.

Chicago is a hub for U.S. futures trading as the home of the Chicago Mercantile Exchange (CME or Merc), and the Chicago Board of Trade (CBOT). The two markets competed from the end of the 1800s until 2007, when the CME Group Inc., the Merc's owner, acquired the CBOT.

CME Group owns the New York Mercantile Exchange (NYMEX), home to WTI futures and other energy contracts, and the exchange's Comex division, a trading hub for contracts on gold and other precious metals. They were acquired in 2008.

IntercontinentalExchange Inc., known as ICE, offers trading in energy, agricultural, and index futures, along with marketplaces for over-the-counter (OTC) commodity contracts.

Additional futures markets are run by NYSE Euronext, the owner of the New York Stock Exchange, as well as the Nasdaq Stock Market, the Chicago Board Options Exchange (CBOE), and other financial companies.

The London Metal Exchange (LME) offers contracts that are more like forwards than futures. Traders can buy and sell aluminum, copper, lead, nickel, tin, and zinc contracts for delivery in three, 15, or 27 months. The three-month prices are a global benchmark for base, or industrial, metals. Derivatives lasting for days and weeks are available, along with spot trading.

Financial forwards generally trade in an OTC market through banks and other financial companies. They arrange contracts for currencies as well as forward rate agreements (FRAs), which allow borrowers to lock in interest rates for loans they will receive later. FRAs resemble interest rate swaps, a type of derivative we'll encounter later.

Separate primary and secondary markets for futures don't exist. The main distinction between new and existing contracts is in the margin payment required to trade them.

Quotations

Futures quotes resemble the stock quotes we saw earlier, except for two main differences. First, you won't find exchange codes because futures contracts trade on one exchange. Second, there's a piece of data you haven't seen before, open interest.

With that in mind, let's look at a crude-oil futures quote from the NYMEX (see Exhibit 10.1). When people refer to the price of oil, they're often citing the value of the most active NYMEX contract. It's worth knowing what they mean.

CLX1: Futures symbol with three components: a contract code, a letter signifying the delivery month, and the last digit of the delivery year.

Contract codes usually are no more than two letters. CL means WTI, the benchmark grade of U.S.

> **DEFINITION:**
> **Open interest**
> Open interest is the number of futures contracts outstanding for a specific expiration month or for all months. The total changes daily as contracts are bought and sold.

```
   CLX1 ↑82.71  +.12  82.70/82.72 1x3
   At 16:59 Vol 343,350 Op 82.57 Hi 84.00 Lo 81.36 OpInt 270,703y
```
Exhibit 10.1 A West Texas Intermediate Crude-Oil Futures Quote

crude. There's a space added after one-letter codes, such as C for corn. The X means November delivery, as each month has a corresponding letter and number. The 1 stands for 2011, as 2 would designate 2012, 3 would mean 2013, and so on through 9 for 2019.

Down arrow: Uptick/downtick arrow, which shows the latest price change.

82.71: Latest price, stated here in dollars per barrel.

+.12: Change on the day, a gain of 12 cents a barrel.

82.70/82.72: Bid and ask prices.

1 × 3: Number of contracts associated with the bid and ask prices. Each contrast represents 1,000 barrels of oil, based on terms the NYMEX sets.

At 16:59: Time of the latest trade. NYMEX oil futures are traded 24 hours a day during the week, so the 24-hour format is more than a convention.

Vol 343,350: Volume, or the number of contracts traded. The total is equivalent to 343.35 million barrels of crude.

Op 82.57, Hi 84.00, Lo 81.36: Opening, high, and low prices for the current day's trading.

OpInt 270,703: Open interest as of the previous day. It's less than the volume in this case because contracts can change hands multiple times during a trading day.

Financial futures are quoted in the same way as commodity contracts. For example, let's look at e-mini futures on the Standard & Poor's 500 Index, traded on the CME (see Exhibit 10.2). These contracts have the e-mini designation because they trade electronically, rather than on an exchange floor, and are one-fifth the value of other S&P 500 futures on the CME.

Though the numbers are bigger than the ones we saw for oil, the format is similar. The first line begins with the four-character symbol, including the expiration month and year. The current price and change on the day follow, along with the bid and ask prices and the number of contracts for each. The second line has the time of the quote, volume, opening price, high and low prices, and open interest.

The difference is the letter "s" that follows the current price. This designates a settlement price, used to calculate the day's gains and losses. All futures have one, including oil contracts.

LME quotes differ from what we have seen, especially because of the symbols used for contracts.

```
ESZ1 ↓1155.00s -2.50  1154.25/1156.25 16x1
At 16:15 Vol 2,865,429 Op 1157.25 Hi 1173.75 Lo 1144.75 OpInt 3,116,403y
```

Exhibit 10.2 A Standard & Poor's 500 Index E-mini Futures Quote

LMAHDSO3 ↓2227.00s -91.00 2225.00/2235.00
At 14:38 Vol 25,510 Op 2321.00 Hi 2321.00 Lo 2223.00

Exhibit 10.3: An Aluminum Three-Month Forward Quote

Some similarities exist as well. Let's look at an aluminum quote and touch on a couple of key points (see Exhibit 10.3).

LMAHDS03: Symbol, consisting of five components. LM designates the LME. AH stands for aluminum, and the exchange has a two-letter code for each metal traded there. D means the price is in dollars. S shows the price is based on reports made to the exchange by members. The 03 means the contract is for delivery in three months.

Vol 25,510: Number of contracts traded. There's no figure for open interest, as the three-month expiration period sets each day's aluminum contracts apart from those traded a day earlier or later.

Let's turn our attention to currency forwards. Quotes for these derivatives differ, as the three-month forward rate for the dollar versus the yen shows in Exhibit 10.4.

JPY3M: Symbol for the forward contract. JPY is the code for the dollar's value in yen, as we saw in Chapter 2, and 3M stands for three months. The number can be anywhere from 1 to 30, and the M can be substituted with a W for weeks or a Y for years. Forward symbols can end in ON for overnight trades, TN for two nights, or SN for three nights.

Down arrow: Uptick/downtick arrow, showing the most recent change in the forward rate.

−11.59: Spread between the three-month forward rate and the spot rate, or the dollar's value against the yen for immediate delivery. The size of the gap reflects interest rates in the United States and Japan and the time until delivery. Longer periods mean wider spreads, and vice versa.

Because these figures are small, the decimal point is two places to the right of where it goes in currency quotes. Here the spread amounts to 0.1159 yen.

> **KEY POINT:**
> Currency forward rates are expressed as spreads. To determine the actual rate, add or subtract the spread from the spot rate.

JPY3M ↓ **-11.59** **-.04** BGN -11.84/-11.34 BGN
At 16:36 Op -11.60 Hi -11.40 Lo -11.77 Close -11.56

Exhibit 10.4 A Yen Three-Month Forward Quote

The minus sign before the spread means you have to subtract it from the spot rate to calculate the forward rate. We can use the rate of 76.33 yen per dollar from Chapter 2 as an illustration. After subtracting the 0.1159, we're left with a three-month forward rate of 76.2141 yen.

–.04: Change on the day. The minus sign means the spread narrowed. The .04 translates into 0.0004 yen.

BGN: Source of the rate spread. BGN stands for Bloomberg generic pricing, which is compiled from data provided by banks and currency-trading firms.

–11.84/–11.34: Bid and ask spreads. The bid spread is wider because this means the forward rate will be lower.

BGN: Source of the bid and ask spreads.

At 16:36: Time of the most recent quote.

Op –11.60, Hi –11.40, Lo –11.77, Close –11.56: Opening, high, and low for the current day's trading, along with the previous day's close. The high is the narrowest spread between the spot and forward rates, and the low is the widest spread.

Three Rs

Futures contracts don't pay interest or dividends even if the underlying asset does. Investors in Treasury note and bond futures, for instance, forgo the payments

they would receive from the securities. Stock-index futures are ineligible for payments on the shares used to compile them.

This means the returns depend on price changes, which can be steep because margins are a few percentage points of the contract's value. The exact percentage figure varies from one future to the next and is set by an exchange, which can adjust margins in response to changes in the pace of price moves and trading. Investors can lose all their money more easily by owning futures rather than the underlying asset. This risk results from leverage. The value of a contract might be 20 times the amount of margin required. If that's the case, then a 5 percent decline wipes out the initial payment.

There's another risk that affects forwards and other OTC derivatives: counterparty risk, or the possibility the other party may not meet its end of the bargain. Buyers may fail to take deliveries, or sellers may fail to make them. Some OTC contracts are administered by exchanges, which minimizes the risk.

Relative-value analysis can focus on time. Investors can compare contracts that expire in different months to determine which ones may be cheap, expensive, or fairly valued. The prices of a contract and the underlying asset provide another basis for comparisons. It's possible to make a profit by buying whichever looks cheaper and short selling the more costly asset.

> **KEY POINT:**
>
> Futures exchanges eliminate counterparty risk by taking the other side of each trade. They sell contracts to buyers and purchase them from sellers, and their clearinghouses ensure that both groups meet their obligations. Clearinghouses play a similar role in many OTC derivatives.

Returns

The leverage that's built into futures provides investors with opportunities and risks. To see this, let's examine the S&P 500 e-mini futures we saw earlier. The contract is valued at $50 times the S&P 500 figure linked to the future. If it's 1,200, for example, then the total is $60,000.

The margin required to buy the futures or to sell them short is as low as $4,000, or 6.7 percent of the total value, based on December 2011 figures. This initial margin is tied to two criteria. The first is whether the investor is designated as a speculator or hedger. The second is whether the contract is new or has changed hands before.

Margin payments are made into an account at the exchange's clearinghouse, which processes trades. The clearinghouse ensures that the investor keeps a maintenance margin, or a minimum amount on deposit. The e-mini has a maintenance margin of $3,200. If losses cause the account balance to fall below that amount, the investor has to provide enough additional money to restore the account to the initial margin amount.

Returns would be based on the entire $60,000. If the S&P 500's value rises by about 7 percent, owners of e-mini contracts can double their money. This works both ways, as a drop of about 7 percent would cost investors an amount that's equal to the initial margin.

Margins have to be maintained daily, so any losses may lead to additional payments that affect returns.

Let's assume the S&P 500 declines 1 percent on a given trading day, and the contract follows suit. If the index future started the day at 1,200, the loss would be 12 points. Multiply by $50, and you have a $600 loss.

If the margin account ends the day with less than $3,200, the investor will have to return the balance to $4,000 to maintain the contract. Otherwise, the exchange automatically sells or buys back the contract, which forces the investor to take a loss. Any added margin payments increase the cost of the contract and reduce the potential returns.

Returns for trades that are made for months or years have another component. Contracts expire at least quarterly, and investors have to exit them before they lapse and buy later ones to keep up their positions. This process is known as a futures roll, as stated earlier, and the difference in price between contracts can add to or subtract from returns.

Futures prices can be transformed into curves, similar to rate curves for bills and yield curves for notes and bonds. When a futures curve slopes upward, prices increase as the time until expiration gets longer. The contract is said to be in contango.

The opposite of contango is backwardation, which exists when prices drop for later contract months rather than rising. Curves for futures in backwardation have a downward slope, like an inverted yield curve. Exhibit 10.5 shows how the shape of the curve for oil shifted in 2008 when crude surged to a record value and then plunged.

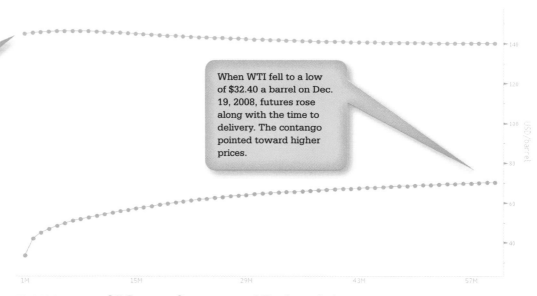

Exhibit 10.5: Oil Futures Contango and Backwardation

July 2008's curve indicated that futures traders saw oil prices falling over time. Five months later, the curve pointed to higher prices. The latter signal was accurate as crude more than doubled in the next 12 months in New York trading.

Risks

Futures magnify the market risk that goes along with any kind of investing. Seven percent swings in the Standard & Poor's 500's value, for instance, can happen in a week or a few days. When they take place, shares of S&P 500 funds are worth 93 percent of their value before the loss. Investors in S&P 500 e-mini futures, by contrast, would lose the full amount of the initial margin payment.

The 100 percent plunge wouldn't occur all at once because exchanges settle contract gains and losses daily through their clearinghouses. Buyers can limit their losses by selling the contracts themselves or choosing not to make additional margin payments, which would cause the exchange to do the selling for them.

Even so, the potential for losing one's entire investment is far greater with futures than with the underlying asset. The same can be said for forwards, which have a comparable amount of leverage built into them.

Otherwise, the risks of owning the contracts are similar to those for the type of investment they represent. Interest rate risk and inflation risk affect note and bond futures though their influence is tied to prices rather than to the value of payments. Business risk, event risk, and industry risk come into play in single-stock contracts, a minor part of the futures market.

With commodity contracts, weather is a concern. Higher-than-normal winter temperatures reduce demand for natural gas and heating oil, fuels used to warm up offices and homes. Droughts, flooding, and other natural disasters harm grains and other agricultural products.

Relative Value

Futures exchanges routinely list multiple contracts, each with a different expiration date. S&P 500 e-mini futures expire quarterly as do the full-sized versions. Crude oil futures in New York expire monthly and are available for each month in the next six years at any given time.

Whatever the schedule might be, there are price gaps between contracts to consider. The numbers will be positive if the futures are in contango and negative if they instead are in backwardation.

Either way, it's possible to analyze price differentials and determine whether they're justified, based on the supply-demand balance and other indicators. This analysis is one way to uncover relative value in the futures market.

Another is to compare the price of a contract and the underlying asset. This can be done with S&P 500 e-mini futures, for example, to see how their values compare with the benchmark stock index. The time until expiration needs to be accounted for along with the dividends paid on S&P 500 stocks.

When the e-mini futures are cheap, it's possible to lock in a profit by buying them and short selling some or all of the index's stocks. When they're comparatively costly, short selling the futures and purchasing the stocks can have the same effect. This trading strategy is known as stock index arbitrage, and it's been around since the 1980s. Knowing where relative value exists is essential to making this strategy work.

Both approaches are similar to those used with notes and bonds. Spreads between contracts that expire in different months or quarters appear on futures curves, as yield spreads are shown on yield curves. The price gap between futures and an underlying asset is another example of a spread.

Relative-value analysis for forwards follows the lead of futures. In the currency market, hedgers and speculators can consider forward curves, forward spreads, and spot-forward spreads in their decision making. Similar data can be located for other contracts.

Options and Warrants

Wimpy still has his hamburger cravings, so let's look at them from another angle. Suppose he wants to

DEFINITION:
Stock index arbitrage

Stock index arbitrage is buying index futures while simultaneously selling shares in the benchmark, or vice versa, to profit from price gaps between them.

lock in the price today for burgers on Tuesday, but he's unsure how many he's going to eat. Perhaps he'll only want two, or maybe he'll be hungrier and have half a dozen.

Futures and forwards won't help Wimpy in that case. Both contracts set the amount that will change hands at the delivery date. He'll have to take all the burgers whether he wants to eat them or not. Instead, he would rather be able to buy six burgers at today's price even if he only wants two on Tuesday.

Let's look at all this from the diner's perspective. Burger sales may be slow on Tuesdays, so the management might be interested in lining up potential buyers. This would ensure the burgers are sold at today's price even if they're cheaper by Tuesday.

This kind of flexibility is available through options, because the contracts set the terms for potential purchases and sales. The key word is potential because the contracts only represent the right to make a deal. There's no obligation to buy or sell, as there is with futures and forwards. Even so, these contracts provide similar opportunities to hedge against or speculate on price moves.

Option buyers can lock in the purchase or sale price, depending on the contract they own. Wimpy would want call options, setting the price to buy burgers on Tuesday. The diner would prefer put options, covering possible sales.

The price of the later purchases or sales is called the strike price because it's where the deal was struck. It's also called the exercise price because it's what the call owner will pay or the put owner will receive by exercising the option.

To lock in the price, Wimpy or the diner would have to pay a premium, as they would for other types of insurance. If the strike price represents a better deal than the market price, then part of the option's premium will reflect the gap between the two. If the burgers sell on Tuesday for $4, the same price we saw earlier, then a call option with a $3.75 strike price will be worth something. That something is 25 cents a burger, known as the option's intrinsic value.

Option prices have a second component: time value, which shows how much investors pay to lock in the purchase or sale price until the contract expires. The longer the time until expiration and the more that a security's or commodity's prices fluctuate, the higher the time value will be for its options.

Let's assume that Wimpy's $3.75 call options are good for two burgers each. They might be quoted at 35 cents, a premium that consists of 25 cents of intrinsic value and 10 cents of time value for each burger. If the diner owned put options with the same $3.75 strike price, they might trade at 5 cents. The puts would have less time value because hamburger prices are more likely to rise than fall, based on history.

The value of the contract would be $7.50, based on the two-burger limit. This is known as the option's notional amount, as the money may or may not change hands when the contract expires.

Wimpy would have to buy three contracts to lock in the price on half a dozen burgers. If he only wants two on Tuesday, he can exercise one of them and let the other two expire. If he decides before Tuesday that he won't eat six burgers, he can sell one or two of the contracts instead of letting them lapse.

If the burgers are only available on Tuesday, Wimpy would have European-style options. They may only be exercised on the expiration date. American-style options are more like offers made by Groupon and other daily-deal websites, as they may be used before the expiration dates. The names reflect historical differences in contract terms between the regions.

Comparing the amount of trading in put and call options would provide insight into the diner's prospects. If puts were more active, then it's likely that investors are locking in the current price because they expect a decline. If calls were more active, the outlook for gains would be brighter.

Here's a real example, using options on the Apple stock we saw earlier. Exhibit 10.6 shows the put-call

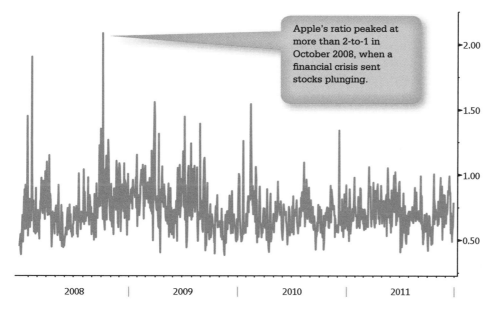

Exhibit 10.6: Apple Put-Call Ratio

ratio, calculated by dividing the number of puts traded each day by the number of calls.

Analysts use put-call ratios to track investor sentiment about markets as well as specific securities. That's possible because there are options on indexes and related investments, such as the Standard & Poor's 500 e-mini futures.

Options are similar to futures in that contracts have standardized terms and trade on exchanges, which set the range of available strike prices, the notional amount, and other criteria. For the kind of customization that goes along with forwards, investors can turn to warrants, another type of agreement that covers the right to buy or sell.

The similarity between warrants and forwards has limits. Companies can create and sell equity warrants and list them on stock exchanges. They can't do the same with forwards, which trade exclusively over the counter.

Warrants can be packaged with bonds or preferred stock to create the equivalent of convertibles with separate securities. In September 2008, billionaire Warren Buffett's company, Berkshire Hathaway Inc., received preferred shares and five-year warrants in Goldman Sachs Group Inc. in return for a $5 billion investment. In 2011, Goldman bought back the preferred. Berkshire kept the warrants, which still had about two and a half years remaining at the time. This wouldn't have been possible if Berkshire received convertible preferred shares in the first place. Having the warrants gave Buffett more flexibility.

Some companies distribute securities known as rights to current shareholders when they need to raise money. Rights are similar to warrants and entitle their holders to buy shares at a preset price. They are issued primarily by non-U.S. companies and can trade on stock exchanges.

Options are more standardized than forwards, warrants, and rights, which means derivatives exchanges play a bigger role in trading. The biggest U.S. options market is run by the CBOE, which the CBOT began in 1973. The exchange went public as CBOE Holdings Inc. in 2010. Options trade alongside futures on the derivatives markets of CME Group and ICE, among other firms.

Customized OTC options are available from securities firms. Their underlying assets, time to maturity, and notional amounts, along with other terms, can differ from those available for exchange-traded contracts.

Quotations

Option quotations vary from one market to the next, as they do for the underlying assets. For that reason, we'll look at two quotes this time around. The first (Exhibit 10.7) is for an option on S&P 500 e-mini futures.

ESV1C: This option ticker symbol has three elements. The first is the contract, identified by the first two letters. ES stands for S&P 500 e-mini options.

The letter and number that follow designate the expiration month and year, using the same convention as futures. Here the letter V stands for October,

```
ESV1C 1155 ↓29.50s -3.75
At 16:15 Op 31.75 Hi 36.25b Lo 26.75 Vol 1,571 OpInt 6,618y
```

Exhibit 10.7 A Standard & Poor's 500 E-mini Call Option Quote

and 1 means 2011 because it's the last digit of the year.

The symbol's fifth character will always be C, for call option, or P, for put option.

1155: Strike price of the option. Combine this number with the C, and you have an option to buy S&P 500 futures at an index value of 1,155.

Down arrow: Uptick/downtick arrow, showing the direction of the last price change.

29.50s: Option premium in index points. The "s" designates a settlement price, as it did with futures. To find the contract's value, multiply the premium by a preset dollar amount, as you would with futures. We learned earlier that e-minis are worth $50 for each index point. Our 1,155 call option is valued at 29.50 times that amount or $1,450.

–3.75: Change on the day, in points. Multiply this value by $50 to determine the day's loss, totaling $187.50.

At 16:15: Time of the quote.

Op 31.75, Hi 36.25, Lo 26.75: Opening, high, and low prices for the current day.

Vol 1,571, OpInt 6,618y: Volume, or the number of contracts traded during the current day, followed by

open interest, or the number outstanding. The "y" next to the open-interest figure means the number is from yesterday, or the previous trading day.

During the trading day, we would see figures like these in the quote: **36.25/36.75, 33×83.** They are bid and ask premiums in points, along with the number of contracts for each. In this case, someone offered to buy 33 e-mini S&P 500 options at a strike price of 1,200. The proposed price is 36.25 index points, or $1,812.50, for each contract. Someone else put 83 options up for sale at 36.75 points each, or $1,837.50.

Now let's look at the second option (see Exhibit 10.8), allowing its owner to purchase shares of Apple stock at $400 each. Some key differences are worth keeping in mind between this quote and the one for the S&P 500 e-mini option.

AAPL US: Ticker and Bloomberg country code for Apple's stock. US refers to U.S. composite trading, covering all the exchanges and electronic markets where shares change hands.

12/17/11: Month, day, and year when the contract expires. Every option has one as every future does. Exchanges set the schedule.

```
▲   AAPL US 12/17/11 P370  $     ↓ 27.30 +2.90 A  I27.15/27.50X   21x3
▼   At 15:57  OpInt 2351  Vol 331 Op 24.90 A  Hi 27.85 Z  Lo 24.15 Q  Prev 24.40
```

Exhibit 10.8 An Apple Put-Option Quote

P370: P as in put option, with a strike price of 370.

27.30: Premium per share of the latest trade. Each option represents the right to buy 100 shares, or a round lot. So, the contract cost the buyer $27.30 times 100, or $2,730.

+2.90: Change on the day.

A: Second letter of the two-letter code for the exchange where the trade was completed. Equity options trade on more than one exchange unlike S&P 500 e-mini options, which belong to the CME. The codes are the same as those for stock, so the A stands for NYSE Amex.

Beyond that, the details are similar to those in other quotes. The first line ends with the bid and ask premiums, the corresponding number of contracts, and the exchange ID. The second line has the time of the quote, open interest, volume, and opening, high, low, and previous closing premiums.

Warrants that trade publicly are quoted in basically the same way as stock. Take a look at this quote (Exhibit 10.9) on JPMorgan Chase warrants, originally awarded to the U.S. government as part of a financial industry bailout.

The /WS designates the security as a warrant, at least on the Bloomberg terminal. For rights, /RT is the comparable code.

What follows the /WS is similar to what we saw with Apple's shares. The 40×12, for example, shows someone wants to buy 4,000 warrants at $9.94 apiece and someone else has 1,200 of them available for sale at $9.99 each.

Three Rs

Price changes are the key to returns on options as they are on futures. Premiums on calls and puts will change as the underlying asset's value rises or falls.

```
▲   JPM/WS US $ ↑  9.95   +.81  N 1s ⊤ 9.94/9.99 N  40x12
▼   At 15:52 Vol 234,654 Op 9.27 P Hi 10.02 P Lo 9.1 N ValTrd  2271420
```

Exhibit 10.9 A JPMorgan Chase Warrant Quote

The demand from investors to lock in the asset's price and the amount of time left until the contract expires affect returns as well.

The risks associated with options are similar to those for futures, starting with leverage. Premiums, like margins, are a small percentage of the underlying asset's market value. It doesn't take much of a price swing in the asset for puts and calls to become worthless. The biggest difference is that option owners can't lose more than the original premium. The contracts don't require additional payments.

Counterparty risk exists for OTC options, available from securities firms. OTC and exchange-traded contracts are subject to any risks that go along with the underlying assets. Economic risk can drag down S&P 500 e-mini options along with the index, for instance.

Relative-value comparisons among options are trickier than we have seen. Investors can't just look at call and put premiums to make comparisons. They have to use an indicator of the potential price swings built into time values. We'll see how that works shortly.

The three Rs for warrants and for rights are similar to those for options. These derivatives can produce higher returns than the underlying assets because of leverage, which adds to their risks. Investors may have less chance to profit from declines as companies' warrants and rights are calls by definition. Though brokerages can create call and put warrants, these securities are sold outside the United States.

Returns

Price changes—in this case, premium changes—are responsible for returns on options. These contracts, like futures, have no interest and dividend payments. This means we need to look more closely at intrinsic value and time value, the components of option premiums.

Intrinsic value can rise or fall over time, depending on what happens to the price of the underlying asset. If the S&P 500 or Apple's stock price rises, their call options will follow suit. If the index or the shares fall instead, the holders of put options will benefit.

Time value reflects the number of days, weeks, or months until the option expires. This falls to zero on the expiration date, when the contract is exercised or becomes worthless. Even so, time value may rise or decline daily as intrinsic value does. The moves depend on how much investors are willing to pay to lock in a strike price.

To see how all this works, let's delve into Apple options. When we looked at Apple's shares, they were quoted at $369.80 each. It wouldn't make sense financially for buyers to pay more than this price or for sellers to take anything less.

This means call options with a strike price of less than $369.80 are worth something because they're a better deal. In other words, they have intrinsic value. The same goes for put options whose strike price exceeds $369.80.

There are $5 gaps between strike prices on Apple options because the stock price is so high. Calls at $365 or lower and puts at $370 or higher, including the one cited earlier, are in the money. This means they have intrinsic value. Options are out of the money when they lack intrinsic value. When the strike price is about the same at the market price, the option is at the money.

Let's assume the $365 call is trading at an $8-a-share premium. The contract is in the money by $4.80 a share, based on the difference between the strike price and the $369.80 market price. You would then subtract the intrinsic value from the premium to calculate the time value, which is $3.20 a share.

A $365 put, by comparison, would have nothing but time value. Investors would rather sell their stock for the market price, $369.80, than for the strike price. The option may trade for only $1 a share, a signal that investors see Apple's stock as more likely to rise than fall.

Changes in intrinsic and time value largely determine returns for option investors. Even though this is the case for short sellers, they can't earn any more than the premiums they collect from selling options. The potential losses can be much greater, depending on what happens to the premiums and asset prices over the life of the contracts.

Suppose an investor sold the $365 call option short at the $8 price. If Apple's shares traded for $390 at expiration, the contract would be valued at $25, more than three times the premium. That would cause a loss on the short sale. Falling prices for the stock would have a similar effect on investors shorting puts.

There's one more return scenario left to consider. Some investors exercise their options rather than exiting the contracts in advance. When that happens, returns are tied to the price of the underlying asset and the premium paid.

In the best-case scenario, locking in the purchase price in advance would be a money-making strategy even after taking the additional expense into account. In the worst-case scenario, savings from the stock purchase would partially offset the 100 percent loss from the option.

Risks

The Apple call option we used for the discussion of returns shows the risks of leverage. The contract's $8 premium is only 2.2 percent of the stock price. Buyers of the company's stock would have to put up far more money, as the Fed limits borrowing for stock purchases to 50 percent of the price paid.

If Apple's shares trade at the $369.80 price on the date of expiration, the stock investor won't have any loss. The owner of the call will lose at least 40 percent, as the premium will shrink to the intrinsic value of $4.80. The loss may reach 100 percent if the investor decides against buying the stock.

This shows the risks posed by leverage, which affects warrants and rights in the same way as options. Contracts traded over the counter have counterparty risk, assuming there isn't an exchange to ensure buyers and sellers meet their obligations.

Though these risks are identical for puts and calls, the same can't be said for market risk. When the underlying asset's price declines, put buyers will benefit and call buyers will suffer. When the asset rises in price, the opposite will be true.

Beyond that, option risks are tied to the asset that the contracts represent. Apple's options are subject to business risk, event risk, and industry risk, like the company's stock and other securities. For owners of bond options, inflation rates and inflation are concerns.

Relative Value

Before we can determine whether options are cheap, expensive, or fairly valued, we need some basis for comparison. Contracts vary by underlying asset, strike price, and month of expiration, among other criteria. There has to be a way to make relative-value judgments regardless of the differences.

That's where implied volatility (vol) comes in handy. The figure is an annual percentage rate that's based on an option's strike price, the asset's market price, the time to expiration, and the interest rate on three-month Treasury bills or comparable debt.

Apple's $365 call option, for example, may have a 30 percent implied volatility. This figure is comparable to percentages for other calls and for puts, as well as the swings in the company's stock price over time. Exhibit 10.10 provides an illustration of how much this can fluctuate.

Comparing the implied volatility of calls can show which strike prices or maturity dates are worth buying or selling. Analyzing calls relative to puts can indicate what investors see ahead for the underlying asset. Relative-value analysis can involve the asset's realized volatility, a historical reading that's based on a specified number of trading days. Someone looking at trends may use a 90-day reading, and someone else focused on more recent swings may go with 10 days instead. Either way, they will see an annual rate that's comparable to implied volatility.

Put-call ratios, such as the one we saw for Apple options, provide insight as well. The ratios are used to analyze markets as well as specific securities and hard assets. A ratio based on S&P 500 puts and calls is used to track sentiment toward U.S. stocks.

Swaps

Wimpy has guided us through the world of derivatives, so let's turn to him once more. Suppose our comic strip character won the right to eat one free hot dog a week for a year through a local contest.

We know Wimpy likes hamburgers more than anything else, so he wouldn't have much use for hot dogs. Even though he could give up the prize, he's too cheap to do that. The cost of one hot dog a week adds up, after all.

Instead, the burger lover makes a deal at the diner. Wimpy finds another customer who's entitled to eat a free burger every week for the next year. He arranges to exchange his hot-dog prize for the other customer's burgers. The dog-for-burger deal is an example of a swap or an exchange between two parties. Financial swaps aren't as simple as Wimpy's agreement because they usually involve exchanges of

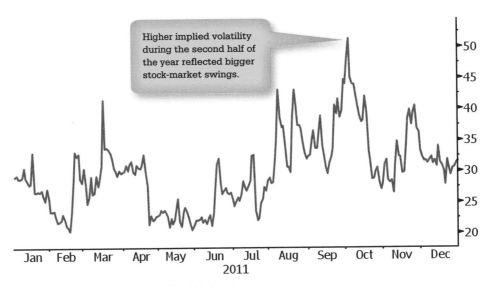

Exhibit 10.10: Apple Implied Volatility

payments rather than food. Yet they can accomplish a similar goal: giving at least one of the parties something they would rather have, like cheaper money.

Swaps have been around since 1981, when International Business Machines Corp. (IBM) and the World Bank signed the first contract. IBM wanted to pay off debt denominated in deutschemarks, Germany's currency at the time, and Swiss francs. The World Bank wanted to borrow in both currencies. The brokerage firm of Salomon Brothers, which later became part of Citigroup, put together the swap. This enabled the bank to borrow in dollars and end

up with marks and francs. The agreement was known as a currency swap because the payments were in different currencies.

Though we'll touch on currency swaps later, we'll focus on two other contracts that are more popular these days. The first is an interest rate swap, or an exchange of payments made at different rates in the same currency. The second is a credit default swap (CDS), or a contract that protects against the risk that a borrower might be unable to pay its debts.

Both swaps are based on notional amounts, which are used to calculate payments. In interest rate swaps, the amounts dictate the size of fixed or floating payments that each party makes to the other periodically. In CDS contracts, they represent the money that would change hands in case of a default.

Interest Rate Swaps

To understand how interest rate swaps work, let's assume the diner wants to borrow money for five years to finance an expansion. The management wants to borrow at a fixed interest rate, so the borrowing cost won't change from year to year. Unfortunately, lenders are so worried that rates may rise that a floating-rate loan is a better deal.

This leaves the diner with three choices. The first is to skip the expansion because the financing is too expensive. The second is to take out the fixed-rate loan and hope for the best. The third is to borrow at the floating rate and make a separate arrangement to obtain the fixed rate.

To carry out the third choice, the diner would have to arrange a five-year interest rate swap. This would mean making payments to another party, usually a bank or securities firm, at a fixed rate. In return, the diner would get payments based on the floating rate.

Let's assume the diner borrowed $5 million for the expansion. The swap contract's value can be set at $5 million even though it's a number pulled out of the air as opposed to a future cash payment. The figure is an example of a notional amount, used to calculate the amount of money changing hands under the contract.

Now suppose the bank loan has a floating rate of Libor plus 2 percentage points, or 200 basis points. The interest rate swap can ensure that the diner receives payments tied to Libor, which would help cover interest on the loan. The payments made would be based on the the fixed rate, set at the time of the swap agreement.

The amount of money changing hands each time is based solely on the gap between the swap rates. If the floating rate is 0.25 of a percentage point lower than the agreed-upon fixed rate, for example, the diner pays the other party 0.25 percent of the $5 million notional amount, or $12,500. If the floating rate is higher, the diner gets paid instead.

Swaps are usually designed to ensure that both sets of payments have the same value when the agreement begins. The gap between the floating and fixed rates determines whether the diner pays or receives money along the way and how much. Because the diner's swap is tied to the loan, they both ought to mature at about the same time. The five-year swap would be ideal for the five-year loan. In some cases, the bank that makes a loan ensures that the timing matches by serving as the swap's other party.

Put this all together, and the diner has what might be called a plain vanilla swap, with conventional terms and conditions. The standards are set by the

STEP-BY-STEP

1. Suppose the diner's fixed-rate payments on the swap are $200,000.
2. Suppose the diner's counterparty owes $250,000 when one of the payments is due.
3. The payments are netted out to determine the gap between them. In this case, the counterparty owes $50,000 more than the diner.
4. Only the net amount changes hands each time. In our example, the diner receives $50,000 from the counterparty.

International Swaps and Derivatives Association (ISDA), an industry trade group that has a set of forms for documenting deals.

The ISDA does its work in the OTC market, where interest rate swaps and similar contracts are arranged and traded. Some trading may move to specialized markets, called swap execution facilities, under terms of the Dodd-Frank Wall Street Reform and Consumer Protection Act signed in 2010. The law requires swaps that are processed by a clearinghouse to be traded on exchanges or the new facilities.

While the five-year swap in our example is typical, other time periods are available, as Exhibit 10.11 shows. We'll take a closer look at the possibilities later in considering relative value.

Forward rate agreements (FRAs), mentioned in the futures and forwards discussion, are single-payment versions of swaps. FRAs specify the number of months until they go into effect and the number of months until they are settled. The gap between the two determines the interest rate that's used to calculate the payments.

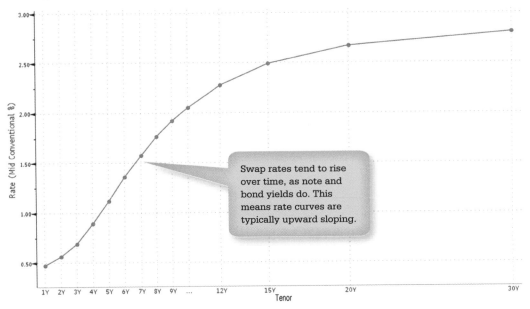

Exhibit 10.11: U.S. Dollar Swap Curve

For example, consider what's described as a 3×6 FRA. The contract begins in three months and ends in six. Six minus three leaves three, so the contract is based on three-month fixed and floating rates. The floating rate for this type of agreement is usually Libor.

Quotations

Interest-rate swap quotes may give you a sense of déjà vu. They resemble what we saw for government bills earlier. Exhibit 10.12 is a sample for a five-year swap contract.

The quote shows a rate rather than a price as bill quotes do. Because swaps change hands in the OTC market, the day's trading, exchange identifiers, and other data—including the uptick/downtick arrow, a fixture with other quotations—are unavailable.

Yet the comparison is too simplistic. The swap quote only tells one side of the story: the fixed rate. You have to know the floating rate, which would be three-month Libor for a plain vanilla swap. With that in mind, let's look at what the quotation provides.

USSWAP5: Swap symbol. US stands for U.S. dollars, and 5 is the number of years until expiration. The

number may be as long as 30, depending on the agreement.

1.0727: Fixed rate for the swap.

–.0693: Change on the day in percentage points. The decline amounts to 6.93 basis points.

ANON 1.0710/1.0752: Bid and ask rates, obtained from anonymous sources. The bid is what a seller would have to pay under the contract, and the ask is what a buyer would receive. That's why the bid is lower, unlike the yields in a bond quote.

At 14:57: Time of the latest quote.

Op 1.1410, Hi 1.1502, Lo 1.0570: Opening, high, and low rates for the current day.

Prev 1.1420: Closing rate for the previous day.

Three Rs

Returns on interest rate swaps will almost inevitably be positive for one party and negative for the other. Rate changes determine which side comes out ahead. When rates rise, the party that's paying the fixed rate is the winner. The amount of money received from the swap increases along with the floating rate. When rates fall, the contract's value tilts in favor of the floating-rate payer.

        USSWAP5 1.0727 −.0693 ANON 1.0710/1.0752
        At 14:57 Op 1.1410 Hi 1.1502 Lo 1.0570 Prev 1.1420

Exhibit 10.12: A Quote for a Five-Year Interest Rate Swap in Dollars

Interest rate risk is the most basic concern for swap investors because it's essentially the same as market risk. Leverage is another risk, as gains and losses on the contracts are based on notional amounts that are far higher than the sums that change hands. There's counterparty risk, as swaps last for years and both parties must survive to meet their contractual obligations.

Relative-value comparisons focus on fixed rates for swaps. The rates are similar to note and bond yields because they vary by time to maturity. They can be tracked historically, compared with each other, or measured against Treasuries and other debt securities with similar maturity dates.

Returns

Swap returns, like those on notes and bonds, are tied to changes in the value of future payments with. There are a couple of key differences. The first is that no principal repayment is required when the contract matures. The notional amount is a number used in calculating payment amounts. The second is that the gap between what the parties owe each other is what counts.

The differential varies in accordance with the terms of the contract and rate changes. Many types of swaps exist besides the one arranged by the diner, and it's worth spending some time on them to understand how they work.

We encountered a currency swap in IBM's deal with the World Bank. Returns on these contracts, known as cross currency swaps, are tied to moves in the foreign exchange market as well as interest rate swings.

Within a single currency, there are swaps in which the floating payments are tied to a published rate that can change overnight. The rate at which U.S. banks borrow from each other through the federal funds market is an example. These contracts are known as overnight indexed swaps.

The gap between Libor and the fixed rates on these swaps, or the Libor-OIS spread, is a gauge of the perceived risk in the financial system. The wider the spread, the more reluctant banks are to lend to each other. The gap soared at the height of the 2008 financial crisis as Exhibit 10.13 shows.

Some swaps have no fixed rate. The parties agree to exchange payments based on different floating rates, such as the three-month Treasury bill rate and three-month Libor. These agreements are known as basis swaps.

Returns on cross currency swaps, overnight indexed swaps, and basis swaps will differ from those on plain-vanilla interest rate swaps because of the way they are put together.

Risks

Interest rate swaps have a total notional amount that is far larger than the global economy, based on data compiled by the Bank for International Settlements (BIS) and the World Bank. The combined value of contracts outstanding at the end of 2010 was $364 trillion, according to the BIS, an organization that helps central banks. Economic output was about $63 trillion worldwide for the year, according to the World Bank.

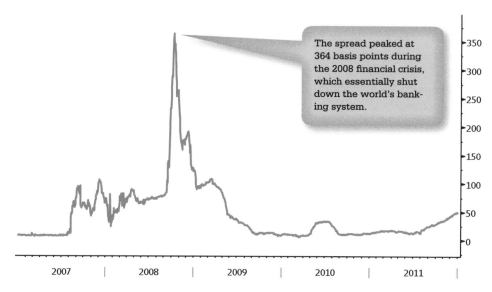

The spread peaked at 364 basis points during the 2008 financial crisis, which essentially shut down the world's banking system.

Exhibit 10.13: Libor-Overnight Index Swap Spread (in basis points)

The comparison shows how much leverage is built into the interest rate swap market. The combined notional amount isn't a real number like the World Bank's figure for gross domestic product, though it's useful as a gauge of the effect that rate swings can have on contracts over time.

Notional amounts highlight the extent of counter party risk in the market. When Lehman Brothers filed for bankruptcy in 2008, the firm defaulted on 66,000 interest rate swaps, which had a total notional amount of $9 trillion. These figures came from LCH.Clearnet, a firm that clears rate swap trades and managed Lehman's default.

Interest rate risk stems from the rate, or rates, used to calculate swap payments. Because floating payments are based on a market rate, interest rate risk is interchangeable with market risk. Basis swaps have a variation, known as basis risk, that reflects the potential for changes in the spread between the contract's market rates.

Relative Value

Interest rate swaps are available for one to 30 years, and there's a fixed rate associated for each maturity. It's possible to depict each rate as a dot on a graph and connect them as Exhibit 10.11 did earlier. The result is a swap curve, a tool that investors can use to judge whether contracts are cheap, expensive, or fairly priced.

Current rates can be compared with historical rates to see how they have changed. Considering what's happened to yields on Treasuries over time, you won't be surprised to know that swap rates have tended to drop. The five-year swap rate was about 1.25 percent at the end of 2011, down from about 5 percent a decade earlier.

Rates at different points on the curve can be translated into swap spreads, another guide to relative value. We can look at the spread between two-year and 10-year interest rate swaps, for example, as we would compare two-year and 10-year Treasury yields.

Treasuries are a third point of comparison. Specifically, the spread between swap rates and yields on Treasury notes or bonds with a similar maturity indicate whether there's more value in the contracts or the securities.

Swap rates provide a way to determine the relative value of individual bonds. Yields and prices on many debt securities are set relative to a benchmark swap rate rather than the rate on a government security. The rate represents a point of comparison in the future.

Credit Default Swaps

Wimpy's diner borrowed from a bank in the interest rate swap example. Let's suppose that the diner sold bonds instead. If its finances later took a turn for the worse, investors in the securities would have reason for concern.

Some investors might sell the bonds and reinvest the money elsewhere. Others might buy a contract that's designed to protect them against the risk that the diner will default, file for bankruptcy, or restructure its finances out of court. This agreement is a credit default swap (CDS), and the possible reasons for a payoff are known as credit events.

Swaps are available on governments and companies, known as reference entities because they aren't directly involved in the contracts. Each swap has a reference obligation, or a note or bond that provides a basis for determining credit events as they occur. Five-year agreements are a benchmark for the market though the time period can range from six months to 10 years. They are denominated in dollars as well as other currencies.

Having "swap" in the name is somewhat of a misnomer. A periodic exchange of payments doesn't occur as with interest rate swaps, cross currency swaps, and other contracts. The protection buyer pays a percentage of the contract's value to the protection seller each year. If the financial position of a government or company is especially weak, the protection buyer may be required to pay an additional amount at the time of the contract. This is known as an upfront payment.

CDSs change hands over the counter through swap dealers, as interest rate swaps do, though many contracts are processed by clearing firms. The ISDA sets

CDS guidelines, and buyers and sellers can customize the agreements.

Rates in the CDS market are quoted in basis points. If a five-year swap is priced at 250, then the buyer must pay 2.5 percent a year. That's $250,000 a year for a standard contract, providing $10 million of protection. In this case, the protection buyer will pay a total of $1.25 million over the life of the swap. Payments are usually made quarterly.

Even though the swaps are a form of insurance or hedging, they can be used to speculate like other types of derivatives. If traders figured Wimpy's diner would go into bankruptcy, they could make a profit by buying a contract without owning any bonds. That's impossible with other types of insurance.

Swap rates tend to rise and fall along with bond yields, so they can signal the perceived safety of a borrower. If swaps on a highly rated country or company are more expensive than those on its peers, the gap suggests the entity has effectively been downgraded by investors even if its credit ratings are unchanged.

Quotations

Let's suppose we wanted to insure the General Electric (GE) bonds cited in Chapter 3. We might look at a CDS quote for GE debt, which would look much the same as what we saw for the interest rate swap. Exhibit 10.14 shows how it might appear.

GECC: Symbol for General Electric Capital, GE's finance unit. Though GE Capital is the reference entity, its status may change because of takeovers and other corporate actions. If the swap covered government debt rather than corporate debt, a country would be the reference entity.

CDS: Identifier for a CDS.

USD: Three-letter code for the dollar, a standard currency for swaps. Contracts can be denominated in euros, yen or other currencies, which makes the USD reference necessary.

SR: Senior debt, specified in most swaps. "Senior" refers to the ranking of bondholders if a company goes into bankruptcy. Contracts can be linked to subordinated debt, which has a lower standing.

5Y: Five years, the most widely used maturity for swaps. Contracts can run from six months to 30 years. The time to maturity for new swaps is the same each trading day as it is with forwards.

242.5Y: Mid price in basis points. This is the percentage of face value that the buyer of a swap has

```
GECC CDS USD SR 5Y    242.5Y as of close 10/12 CMAN
               Bid 234.1  Ask 251.0
```

Exhibit 10.14 A GE Capital Five-Year Credit Default Swap Quote

> **KEY POINT:**
>
> CDS buyers profit when a company's financial position worsens. This makes the contracts similar to put options on stocks, which rise in value when the share price declines.

to pay yearly to keep the contract in place. In this example, 242.5 basis points would amount to 2.425 percent.

To figure out the dollar amount of the payment, we have to know the contract's size. A typical CDS may cover $10 million of debt. Assuming that's the case here, we can calculate what 2.425 percent of $10 million would be. That works out to $242,500 a year. When a borrower's ability to pay its debt is in doubt, swap buyers may have to make an upfront payment.

As of close 10/12: Time of the latest quote. The spread is from the previous day, as quotes during the day are available only through specialized services.

CMAN: Price source. CMAN stands for the New York office of CMA Datavision, a provider of over-the-counter trading data for the credit markets.

Bid 234.1 Ask 251.0: Bid and ask prices in basis points.

There's one more detail omitted from the quote that's worth highlighting: the projected recovery rate, or percentage of face value that bondholders would receive if the borrower went bust. A 40 percent rate is typically used.

Three Rs

CDSs resemble put options because they increase in value as the underlying asset's price falls, and vice versa. Returns for protection buyers are based on price changes. Sellers depend on the swap's payments, made over time or upfront, for their returns. They stand to make money as long as the reference entity, either a government or a company, meets its debt obligations.

Leverage and counterparty risk come into play with these contracts as they did with interest rate swaps. The $10 million in our earlier example can be defined as a notional amount even though it's payable in the case of credit event. The buyer and seller of protection must stay in business to meet their obligations. That's especially true for swaps traded without the benefit of clearinghouses, which tally daily gains and losses on the contracts and require margin payments similar to those made on exchange-traded futures and options.

Because contracts are available for periods other than five years, it's possible to create CDS curves and track CDS spreads, which help investors decide what's cheap, expensive, or fairly valued. These curves and spreads are similar to the ones for government bonds, corporate bonds, and interest rate swaps, and provide a basis for comparing these investments. Exhibit 10.15 displays a curve for contracts on GE Capital's debt.

Returns

There are two sides to returns on CDSs, as we saw with other derivatives. Let's start with the protection buyer and then turn our attention to the

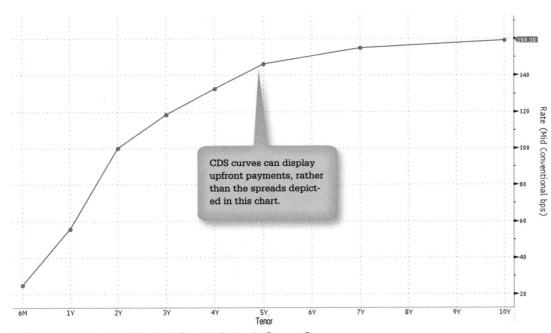

Exhibit 10.15: GE Capital Credit Default Swap Curve

protection seller. The buyer is anticipating the entity's business or financial position will worsen, making a credit event more likely. This puts the buyer in a similar position to the owner of put options. The biggest difference between the derivatives is that swaps have no intrinsic value. Because they are a form of insurance, the buyer may end up with nothing but years of protection if the contract isn't sold before expiration.

The seller will make money on the swap payments as long as the government or company manages to avoid default, bankruptcy, or restructuring. More leeway exists than for a put option, where small changes in an asset's value can lead to losses that exceed the initial premium. Then again, any increase in the swap rate would hurt the seller's returns while the contract is in effect.

Either way, the key point to understanding returns is that CDSs are a bet against the country or company that serves as the reference entity. The wager pays off in extreme cases. Otherwise, changes in CDS rates influence the contract's value.

Risks

Financial markets sometimes force us to think differently about risk than we normally do. Faster economic growth is a risk for investors in notes and bonds. Higher asset prices are a risk for short sellers, as well as owners of put options.

We'll have to get into the same mind-set to understand the risks of CDSs. Their value is likely to fall as the pace of economic growth accelerates, lifting government tax revenue and corporate profits. Increases in the price of bonds and other assets are a risk, assuming they occur because a reference entity is moving toward a stronger financial position.

We have to look at credit risk and default risk differently than we did with money market debt, notes, bonds, and bank loans. These risks are more like opportunities. The greater the credit risk, the more value there is in the contracts' insurance. Defaults lead to swap payoffs, which compensate for losses on the entity's bonds at a minimum.

Business risk, event risk, and industry risk affect swaps tied to corporate debt though they're the opposite of what they are for the underlying securities. Anything that would cause the price of notes and bonds to fall would increase the value of the contracts because they protect against a worst-case scenario.

Relative Value

The shortest standard CDS agreements last six months and the longest run 10 years as noted earlier.

In addition to the five-year benchmark, contracts lasting one year, two years, three years, four years, and seven years are available. That adds up to eight maturity dates, more than enough to take the connect-the-dots approach one more time and come up with swap curves. They are available for individual reference entities, be they governments or companies.

Tracking the history of any swap rate plotted on the curve is a way to find relative value. Another is to calculate the spread between two CDS rates and to study where it's been over time.

Comparisons between swaps and corporate notes are worthwhile. It's possible to use the swap curve to calculate the rate for a contract that matches the maturity of a specific note. From there, an investor can decide if the swap is worth buying or avoiding.

Much of this should have a familiar ring. The analysis is similar to what's performed for government and corporate notes and bonds and their variations. It resembles the relative-value approach for interest rate swaps. Even as the investments change, the process of deciding which ones are cheap, expensive, or fairly priced stays much the same.

Video:
Credit-default swap rates, curves & spreads & comparisons with bonds
www.wiley.com/go/bvgfinancialmarkets

Test Yourself

Answer the following multiple-choice questions:

1. The counterparty for a futures trade is:
   a. Another investor.
   b. A securities firm.
   c. An exchange.
   d. All of the above.
   e. a and b only.

2. For futures, the equivalent of an inverted yield curve is:
   a. Contango.
   b. Backwardation.
   c. A futures roll.
   d. All of the above.
   e. a and b only.

3. These are the components of an option's price:
   a. Time value.
   b. Intrinsic value.
   c. Put-call value.
   d. All of the above.
   e. a and b only.

4. Categories of interest-rate swaps include:
   a. Cross currency swaps.
   b. Overnight indexed swaps.
   c. Basis swaps.
   d. All of the above.
   e. a and b only.

5. Credit-default swaps guard against the risk of default on a:
   a. Reference entity.
   b. Reference bond maturity.
   c. Reference security only.
   d. All of the above.
   e. a and b only.

Answers: 1. c; 2. b; 3. d; 4. e; 5. a

CHAPTER 11

Mutual Funds and Exchange-Traded Funds

Peter Lynch, Bill Miller, and Bill Gross are among the investors who made names for themselves in the fund industry. Lynch headed the Fidelity Magellan mutual fund for 13 years and posted an average annual return of 29 percent. Miller's returns at his flagship fund, Legg Mason Capital Management Value Trust, beat the Standard & Poor's 500 Index for 15 straight years. Under Gross's leadership, the Pimco Total Return bond fund grew into the world's largest mutual fund, a distinction that Fidelity Magellan once held.

Yet the fund industry may owe a bigger debt to the work of a university professor, Harry Markowitz, than to any of these fund managers. Markowitz's research showed that owning the right mix of assets would allow investors to increase returns without taking on more risk.

Markowitz published his results during the 1950s, when he taught at the University of Chicago. The studies became the basis for what's known as modern portfolio theory, and they earned him a Nobel Prize in economics.

By defining the relationship between risk and returns, Markowitz helped make a case for diversification. Rather than owning one stock, own 20, 50, or maybe 100. This may earn you more money and cushion the blow if one holding does poorly.

By investing in a fund, you can have stakes in 20, 50, or 100 companies and spare yourself the time and expense of buying them one by one. Funds offer similar opportunities to diversify in money market securities, government bonds, corporate bonds, municipal bonds, mortgage-backed debt, preferred stock, convertible securities, bank loans, hard assets, master

> ### DEFINITION:
> **Diversification**
> Diversification means putting your investment eggs in many baskets rather than a few. This reduces the risk that losses on any one holding will cause the value of your assets to plunge.

159

limited partnerships (MLPs), and real estate investment trusts (REITs).

Some funds routinely invest in more than one type of asset. Balanced funds are an example. They own stocks, bonds, and cash equivalents in percentages that are set by the fund company. A balanced fund may keep 60 percent of assets in stocks and the other 40 percent in bonds and cash.

Whatever the assets may be, they are owned by all of the investors as a group, or mutually. It isn't like a manager buys a stock or bond and then assigns some percentage of the holding to each owner. That's why this type of investment is commonly called a mutual fund.

Many funds have one or more managers who decide what to buy, hold, and sell at any given time. They are called actively managed, or active, funds because someone at the fund is doing the decision making. Active funds have been around in the U.S. since 1924, when the Massachusetts Investors Trust began.

Other funds are built to track the performance of stock, bond, and commodity indexes. They're known as passively managed, or passive, because the fund company must follow the lead of the index provider. The manager's main responsibility is to keep the fund holdings in line with the index's makeup.

The Vanguard 500 Index Fund, introduced in 1975, was the first passive fund. The fund owns shares of each company in the Standard & Poor's 500 Index, and its investment in each one depends on its standing in the index. If a company represents 1 percent of the S&P 500's value, for example, then the fund will invest 1 percent of its money in the stock.

Passive funds are described as index funds because of their ties to a specific index, or benchmark. They don't have to own every security in the index to fit the category, either. When it would be too costly or impractical to buy them all, a fund can own some of them instead.

Where you buy and sell shares of a fund, and when you're able to do so, depends on how it's organized. There are three basic categories: open-end funds, closed-end funds, and exchange-traded funds (ETFs).

Open-end funds are the biggest part of the industry. The term refers to the number of shares outstanding, which changes daily. The fund's manager sells shares and buys them back each business day after the close of trading. The trades are made with fund companies or through so-called supermarkets run by Charles Schwab, Fidelity, Vanguard, and other firms.

All buying and selling is done at net asset value (NAV), or the total value of a fund's assets, divided by the number of shares outstanding. If a fund has $1 billion of assets and 100 million shares, for example, the net asset value is $10 a share. "Net" means the value accounts for any borrowing done by the fund.

Closed-end funds trade on exchanges rather than through fund companies. There's a primary market, where shares of newly created funds are first sold, and a secondary market, where they trade afterward. This

> **KEY POINT:**
>
> Some index funds own a cross section of securities in their benchmarks rather than all the components. This approach can reduce trading costs and liquidity risk. The sampling is designed to track the index as closely as possible.

is the smallest fund category in the United States, and the oldest. The first closed-end fund, the Boston Personal Property Trust, was formed in 1893.

Market prices usually differ from NAV. If the $1 billion fund mentioned previously is a closed-end fund, its shares may trade at $9 or $10.50 rather than the $10 NAV. The lower price is $1 less than the NAV, giving buyers a 10 percent discount. The higher price is 50 cents more than the NAV, amounting to a 5 percent premium.

Exchange-traded funds (ETFs) are a cross between the other two types. They are similar to closed-end funds because shares are bought and sold on exchanges as their name implies. Even so, the number of shares can vary as it does for open-end funds. Institutions can swap assets for shares, and vice versa, which keeps the stock price in line with the NAV.

ETFs arrived in the United States a century after closed-end funds. The first was the trust behind the Standard & Poor's Depositary Receipt (SPDR or Spider), which tracks the S&P 500 and is among the most actively traded ETFs today. While most ETFs own stocks as the SPDR Trust does, some focus on bonds or commodities instead.

The popularity of ETFs led to the development of exchange-traded notes (ETNs), whose returns reflect the performance of a market index. ETNs are linked to commodities, currencies, and other assets. They are debt obligations of financial companies, so buyers take counterparty risk along with the risks of investing in the market that ETNs track. They don't pay interest, either.

ETFs and ETNs are examples of exchange-traded products, or ETPs. Another example is exchange-traded commodities (ETCs), a category that's sometimes used for ETFs and ETNs tied to gold, oil, and other raw materials.

Video:
Mutual-fund prices vs NAV: open-end, closed-end & ETF,
www.wiley.com/go/bvgfinancialmarkets

Passive funds, like SPDRs, are the rule for ETFs and other ETPs because managers have to disclose their holdings so institutions can trade with them. Closed-end funds, on the other hand, are actively managed. Open-end funds can be active or passive.

Active funds use indexes as a benchmark, or way to gauge their performance. Managers seek to gain more than the benchmark when prices are rising, or lose less when they're dropping. Few are able to do this consistently because funds have a handicap: fees and expenses. The managers have to beat the benchmark by a wide enough margin to cover the costs and still come out ahead.

Quotations

Open-end fund quotes lack many details that we're used to seeing. Exhibit 11.1, an example for the Vanguard 500 Index Fund, makes that clear.

VFINX US $ NAV **107.96−3.27** Purch Prc **107.96** As of Sep21

Exhibit 11.1: A Quote for the Vanguard 500 Index Mutual Fund

VFINX: Symbol for the fund. Open-end funds traded in the United States have five-letter symbols, and the fifth letter is always X to show their status.

US: Two-letter country code.

$: Dollar-denominated security.

NAV 107.96: NAV of each fund share as of the previous day.

−3.27: Latest change in net asset value.

Purch Prc 107.96: Purchase price of the fund's shares as of the previous day. Vanguard sells every share of the Vanguard 500 that investors want to buy, and vice versa, after the close of trading each day. The trades are made at each day's closing NAV.

As of Sep21: Date of the most recent price.

Quotations on closed-end funds and ETFs, by contrast, have all the details provided in stock quotes. This makes sense, as their shares trade in the same markets as common stock. General American Investors Inc., a closed-end fund that has been investing since 1927, is a good example (see Exhibit 11.2).

The stock symbol, exchange codes, dollar sign, uptick-downtick arrow, share price, change on the day, bid and ask, time, volume, open, high, and low are all here.

That's the case for the S&P 500 SPDR as well. Exhibit 11.3 shows what you'll see when looking at shares of this fund.

Except for the size of the numbers, the SPDR quote looks the same as the General American quote or a quote on Apple.

Three Rs

Fund investors don't have to write checks to cover fees and expenses, including the manager's salary. Instead, those costs come out of returns, which otherwise

 GAM US $ ↑ **23.56** +.58 P N23.52/23.60N   5x2
At 16:15 Vol 27,322 Op 23.04 N Hi 23.56 P Lo 22.73 P ValTrd 632292

Exhibit 11.2: Quote for the General American Investors Closed-End Fund

SPY US $ ↑ 112.08   -4.55 P 2s X 112.07/112.08 Z 12x13
At 14:59 Vol 352,629,207 Op 113.25 B Hi 114.21 T Lo 111.67 Z ValTrd 39981.249m

Exhibit 11.3: Quote for the SPDR Standard & Poor's 500 Exchange-Traded Fund

are tied to price changes and income from the fund's investments. The costs may lead to negative returns for investors even in periods where the fund made money.

The risks of fund investing are linked mainly to its holdings. Additional risks go along with having someone else manage your money. The manager may pick poorly performing investments or change strategies through daily buying and selling.

Relative-value analysis is made more difficult because a fund's assets tend to shift over time. A stock that may be among its biggest and cheapest holdings in one period, for example, may be gone the next because it's become too expensive for the manager to hold. This can affect the yields or financial ratios used to compare a fund with itself or its peers.

Returns

Fund returns primarily depend on the performance of the securities or hard assets they own. If the holdings rise in value, the returns will be positive, and vice versa. Interest payments are part of the equation for bond funds as dividends are for stock funds.

There's another component of returns that mainly affects closed-end funds: price changes relative to NAV. If a fund's stock moved to a 5 percent premium from a 10 percent discount, for instance, that would add to returns. A swing in the other direction would do the opposite.

That's the plus side of returns. The minus side consists of fund fees and expenses. Some funds require the payment of an upfront fee, known as a load, when investors buy shares. The load is a set percentage of the amount invested. Others are no-load funds, which means they don't impose this charge.

Even if investors avoid loads, they can't get away from paying the fund's operating costs. Managers and their staff don't work for free. There are expenses related to buying and selling the fund's stock and its holdings. Back-office charges must be paid. Marketing and distribution costs are part of the mix, and many funds cover them by imposing a 12b-1 fee, named for a U.S. rule that authorized the charge.

Active funds are more costly than passive funds as a group. An active fund's annual expenses may equal 1.5 percent of assets, for example. For the cheapest index funds, the expense ratio is less than 0.1 percent.

In other words, paying someone to decide which stocks, bonds, or other assets are worth owning can cost far more than turning over the decision making to an index provider as passive funds do. The higher

STEP-BY-STEP: PRICE AND NAV

1. Shares of a closed-end fund rise to $22 from $20 during a year. The increase amounts to $2, or 10 percent.
2. The NAV climbs to $19 a share from $18 in the same period. The gain is $1, or half of the stock's advance.
3. The fund's premium to NAV widens to $3, or 16 percent, from $2, or 11 percent. The larger premium accounts for the other half of the increase.

the fees and expenses, the more difficult it is for a fund's manager to beat its benchmark.

Risks

The risks of investing in a fund depend primarily on its holdings as the returns do. Bond funds take on interest rate risk and credit risk with their investments. Stock funds deal with business risk and industry risk.

Actively managed funds pose another threat, known as manager risk. It's the possibility that a manager will steer the fund away from its strategy, as defined by the fund company, or will fail to deliver acceptable returns.

Legg Mason's Value Trust illustrates this kind of risk. The fund's returns under Miller beat those of the S&P 500 each year from 1991 through 2005. During the next three years, Value Trust trailed its benchmark by such a wide margin that the fund was among the worst performers in its category.

By November 2011, when Miller said he would retire as manager, most of the fund's advantage over the index had been lost. Exhibit 11.4 shows Value Trust's rise and fall, starting in 1991.

Miller's approach to value led him to invest in companies such as Amazon.com Inc., eBay Inc, and Google Inc. that many of his peers viewed as growth stocks. This kind of shift is described as style drift. He also bought stakes in Citigroup Inc., Eastman Kodak Co., and other companies that later plunged in value. Anyone invested in an S&P 500 index fund, rather than Value Trust, would have avoided being hurt by his decisions.

Passive funds have a different risk, called tracking error, in which they fail to keep pace with their benchmark indexes. The error can happen because of the fund's investments, expenses, and timing of cash flows, among other reasons.

Relative Value

What makes a fund's shares look cheap? What makes them expensive? The answer lies with its holdings, which allow you to classify the fund and determine its relative value. This process involves analysis similar to what we looked at earlier for individual securities.

Let's start with stock funds. They can be large-cap, mid-cap, or small-cap, like companies. The appropriate category depends on the average market value of the companies in which they're invested. The same approach can determine whether the fund's holdings are domestic or international, whether the manager favors growth stocks or value stocks, and whether its industry stakes differ from those of its benchmark.

These distinctions make it possible to compare a fund against itself and its peers. Average price-earnings ratios (P/Es), dividend yields, and other gauges are a basis for these kinds of comparisons.

Money market funds and bond funds are categorized by the securities they hold: government, corporate, municipal, mortgage-backed, and so on. The average maturity of their holdings is used to classify them as short-term, intermediate-term, or long-term. The distinction between domestic and international funds applies.

KEY POINT:

Actively managed funds can fail to follow their stated investment strategy because of a manager's decision making. Passively managed funds can fail to track their benchmarks.

1200

1000

800

Value Trust
Total Return

600

S&P 500
Total Return

400

Value Trust suffered
bigger losses than most
of its peers during the
worst bear market since
the Great Depression.

200

'91 '92 '93 '94 '95 '96 '97 '98 '99 '00 '01 '02 '03 '04 '05 '06 '07 '08 '09 '10 '11

Exhibit 11.4: Legg Mason Value Trust versus Standard & Poor's 500 Index

Average yields provide a basis to determine whether these funds are cheap or expensive. Indicators of the fund's credit risk and interest rate risk, such as average maturity, are used in the analysis as well.

Alternative Funds

Commodities and real estate are alternative assets because they aren't stocks, bonds, or cash. Alternative investing involves funds whose strategies go beyond buying and holding publicly traded securities.

Hedge funds are private investment partnerships that are free to sell short and to use derivatives in pursuing their strategies. Private equity funds buy stakes in companies and often take them over with borrowed money. Venture capital funds provide money and expertise to newer companies that have not become public. There's also angel investing, done by individuals rather than funds.

These days, hedge funds are far different than they were when Alfred W. Jones started the first one in 1949. Back then, the funds focused on hedging by buying the shares of some companies and betting against others at the same time.

Many of today's hedge funds follow a similar strategy to Jones's fund. Others don't hedge at all. Their investments aren't limited to stocks either. What these funds have in common is that they can take money from a limited number of institutions and wealthy individuals, have few restrictions on their decision making, and disclose little about themselves.

Private equity funds invest in privately held companies, mainly by buying stock. Their strategies include leveraged buyouts (LBOs), in which they take over public companies with borrowed money. The target's assets are used as collateral for the loans, and funds put up some money as equity. Companies are often overhauled and taken public again, enabling funds to reap profits from their investments.

Most funds are set up as limited partnerships, a form of organization that's similar to the MLPs we encountered in the energy industry. A private equity firm serves as the general partner, raising money and making investments. Firms set up new funds every few years, and each one usually lasts about a decade.

Business development companies (BDCs), authorized by Congress in 1980, are similar to private-equity funds. BDCs focus on financing for smaller companies. They are passthrough entities, like MLPs and REITs, and must pay out at least 90 percent of their profits as dividends each year to maintain that status. Some BDCs are publicly traded.

Venture capital funds make investments in newer companies that aren't in a position to raise money through the equity or debt markets. These funds provide financing to help the companies grow and business expertise needed to manage their development.

Technology companies often depend on venture capital financing in their early stages. Apple Inc., Amazon.com Inc., Genentech Inc., and Google Inc. are among companies that raised money from funds before going public. Kleiner Perkins Caufield & Byers and Sequoia Capital, based in California's Silicon Valley, are among the funds that specialize in technology investing.

Angel investments are a fallback for companies too small for venture capital. Wealthy individuals are the angels, providing companies with funding and management advice. Angels can act on their own or as part of a larger group.

Hedge funds are the most diverse category because they can pursue any one of several strategies. Some involve high degrees of risk, and others are much safer bets. Some range across stocks, bonds, commodities, and currencies, and others are more market specific.

Global macro strategies are the biggest-picture approach to investing. Managers of macro funds determine the potential for changes in the global economy and markets. They invest in stocks, bonds, commodities, or currencies to profit from those views, and use leverage to magnify their bets.

George Soros, who co-founded and managed the Quantum Fund, became a billionaire by succeeding with this strategy. He earned $1 billion for his investors when the United Kingdom effectively devalued the pound in September 1992. Soros's funds bet the currency would decline, and he became known as the man who broke the Bank of England.

Equity hedge funds can have a long bias or short bias, which means they can focus on owning stocks or betting against them. Long-biased funds more closely resemble mutual funds and ETFs in their strategy. Short-biased funds rely on bets against securities, made through short sales.

Long-short equity funds are among those whose investing resembles Jones's original strategy. These funds buy some stocks and bet against others. They include 130/30 funds, which use leverage to invest 130 percent of assets in long positions and to make short sales totaling 30 percent of assets. Other funds range from 120/20 to 150/50, depending on the percentage of assets they buy and sell short. The 150/50 reflects a short-sale limit under U.S. rules.

There are market neutral funds, a type of long-short fund that buys securities and sells them short in equal amounts. The manager might pursue this strategy by buying shares of one company in a given industry and betting against another. The funds are designed to minimize market risk, enabling them to make money whether prices are rising or falling.

Another strategy that has a similar goal is arbitrage, or buying a security that's cheap and selling short a similar security that's more expensive. Some arbitrageurs buy shares of takeover targets and bet against the acquirer. Others buy convertibles and sell short the underlying shares, or vice versa.

Convertible arbitrage is among the strategies pursued by funds that own debt, as opposed to equity. Others specialize in different versions of arbitrage or in mortgage-backed or asset-backed debt.

Managed-futures funds bet on or against commodities, currencies, bonds, and stocks through the use of futures contracts. The managers who run them are called commodity trading advisers, and their strategies are largely designed to identify and profit from market trends.

These categories aren't all-inclusive. Equity funds can be distinguished by their preference for growth or value stocks or by the regions in which they invest. Emerging market equity and debt funds can be considered separately. There are funds that seek to profit from market volatility or price swings. Funds can pursue two or more strategies at the same time.

Investors can put money into more than one strategy through funds of funds, which invest in a number of hedge funds. The fund-of-funds approach is especially expensive, as investors must pay fees to the fund's manager and to the firms running the hedge funds in which it has stakes.

Hedge fund managers aren't the only investors using these strategies. Mutual funds and ETFs follow the long-short, market neutral, arbitrage, and managed-futures approaches, among others.

Quotations

Alternative-fund quotations can amount to nothing more than a ticker symbol, a net asset value per share and a date when the NAV was disclosed. Anyone seeking additional details must go to more specialized databases, available on the Bloomberg terminal and from other providers. Only accredited investors, defined as institutions and wealthy individuals in the U.S. and elsewhere, are permitted to view them.

Managers of these funds are a different story because some are publicly traded. Apollo Global Management LLC, Blackstone Group LP, and KKR & Co. LP are among them. Blackstone and KKR are organized as MLPs as the LP at the end of their names indicates.

Exhibit 11.5 shows a quote on Blackstone. There's no difference, aside from the numbers, between this quote and the ones we saw before for Enterprise Products, Prologis, and Apple. Prices, volume, exchange codes, and other details in the first and second lines are identical.

Three Rs

Alternative funds have varying goals for returns. Some of them are designed to pursue higher returns than an investor can obtain from stocks and bonds. Others look for absolute returns, or gains regardless of how markets are faring. Either way, the funds charge higher fees than mutual funds and ETFs, which reduce the amount of money that goes to investors.

Liquidity risk is especially prominent with these funds because managers routinely set limits on investors' ability to sell stock. Leverage is another noteworthy risk, especially for private equity funds, which depend on borrowed money in LBOs. Investors bear risks tied to the funds' holdings, and they vary in accordance with the assets bought or sold short.

Relative-value analysis can be more challenging for funds than for other investments because the data used in comparisons aren't publicly available. Only accredited investors are legally permitted to obtain access.

Returns

Changes in the NAV of an alternative fund's shares determine returns. Fund shares don't pay dividends though payouts on the funds' investments affect

BX US $ ↑ 13.6 -.41 Y 1s ↑ 13.59/13.6 N 14x380
At 15:57 Vol 2,136,515 Op 14.1 ↑ Hi 14.2 D Lo 13.57 Y ValTrd 29568918

Exhibit 11.5: A Blackstone Group LP Unit Quote

returns by increasing NAVs. Interest payments have the same effect for funds investing in debt.

The use of leverage, a common practice for hedge funds in addition to private equity funds, can help investors make money. Hedge funds borrow money to make their investments and trade derivatives, which have leverage built into them.

Returns on funds reflect their higher fees. Hedge funds collect management fees and a percentage of investment earnings as a rule. Investors may be required to pay 2 percent of assets under management along with 20 percent of profits every year, which is known as a 2-and-20 arrangement. Though some funds have lower fees, the most popular and successful ones cost more.

Private equity fund fees are similar to those for hedge funds except that the manager has to exceed a minimum rate of return before receiving a percentage of profits. The threshold is the fund's hurdle rate, and the earnings payout is known as carried interest.

Alternative funds' ability to charge so much for their services is based on their performance. During the 2000s, hedge fund returns tracked gains in Treasuries even though many of them were invested in stocks and not bonds. Exhibit 11.6 makes the comparison.

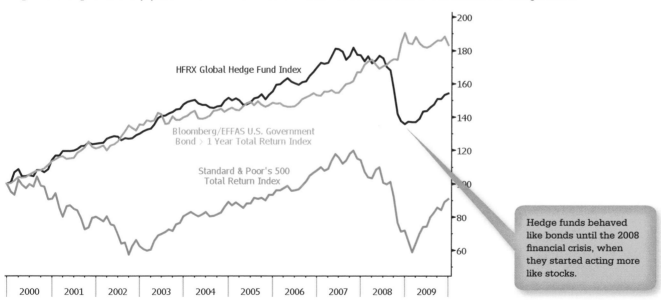

Exhibit 11.6: Hedge Funds versus U.S. Stocks and Bonds

Funds don't always deliver on the promise of absolute returns. In 2008, the hedge fund index shown in the chart dropped 23 percent. The decline ended a decade-long string of annual gains. The indicator fell again in 2011 and did worse than stocks and bonds.

Risks

Alternative investments carry a high degree of liquidity risk. Hedge funds limit investors' ability to withdraw money, especially through initial lock-up periods that may last a year or two. Funds sometimes cut off withdrawals after steep losses, a tactic designed to give themselves time to rebound.

Borrowing by hedge funds and private equity funds increases the potential for investment losses as well as profits. Fund managers face the risk that a holding's interest or dividends, or a company's earnings and cash flow, may fail to cover the payments required on the borrowed funds.

Business risk, industry risk, event risk, and bankruptcy risk affect alternative funds that invest in companies. The risks are high for venture capital funds, as well as angel investors. The companies they support are not as established as those that are publicly traded. Many of them are likely to fail over time.

Funds that invest in debt securities pose interest rate risk, inflation risk, reinvestment risk, credit risk, and default risk for investors. The last two risks are most notable for hedge funds specializing in distressed securities, which are the bonds and shares of companies that face business or financial difficulty.

One more risk that goes along with alternative funds can be described as a lack of transparency. Investors in stocks, bonds, currencies, and commodities usually can find the market value of their holdings in real time. Fund investors don't have that opportunity, as NAVs and other data are provided only periodically.

Relative Value

Alternative fund investing has more to do with getting behind a manager and a strategy, and being willing to pay the fees required to profit from them, than looking for shares that are cheap, expensive, or fairly valued. The data needed to make relative-value judgments can be elusive, especially for those who don't qualify as accredited investors.

Historical returns are more widely available, which makes relative performance easier to judge than relative value. There are indexes available for fund categories and strategies, which make it possible to determine how a specific fund is faring compared with its peers. We'll look at some of these indexes in the next section.

Test Yourself

Answer the following multiple-choice questions:

1. These types of mutual funds can trade at prices that differ from asset value per share:
   a. Exchange-traded fund
   b. Closed-end fund
   c. Open-end fund
   d. All of the above.
   e. a and b only.

2. Mutual funds may deviate from their strategy because of:
   a. Manager risk.
   b. Style drift.
   c. Tracking error.
   d. All of the above.
   e. a and b only.

3. Mutual funds cover their expenses by:
   a. Imposing annual fees on investors.
   b. Keeping a portion of their profits.
   c. Earning income on their investments.
   d. All of the above.
   e. a and b only.

4. Alternative funds cover their expenses by:
   a. Imposing annual fees on investors.
   b. Keeping a portion of their profits.
   c. Earning income on their investments.
   d. All of the above.
   e. a and b only.

5. Alternative funds in this category buy entire companies:
   a. Hedge funds.
   b. Private equity.
   c. Venture capital.
   d. All of the above.
   e. a and b only.

Answers: 1. e; 2. e; 3. c; 4. d; 5. b

12

Indexes Revisited

When you hear about how commodity markets are doing, chances are that you won't find out the actual prices at which raw materials trade. Instead, you'll be told all about commodity futures. That's because the contracts change hands more actively and price data are more readily available in real time.

It's the same for indexes that track commodities as a group. Though you may recall the spot index cited earlier, the most widely followed indicators are based on the prices of futures. Bloomberg has a series of these indexes as do Standard & Poor's and other providers.

This is one example of how derivatives-based indexes shed light on what's happening in financial markets. Barometers linked to options provide insight into the kind of price swings that investors expect for stocks and other investments. Credit default swap (CDS) indexes show the amount of risk they see in lending money to countries and companies.

Indexes based on fund performance are helpful. They make it possible to see how managers compare with their peers rather than the market in which they invest. These indicators classify funds by type, investment style, geography, and other criteria, which makes for fair comparisons.

We'll look at fund indexes later. For now, let's focus on those tied to derivatives.

Futures

Commodity futures indexes have existed for longer than some types of derivatives. In 1956, the Commodity Research Bureau (CRB) began producing an index. Dow Jones got started even earlier. Goldman Sachs brought out a commodity gauge in 1991 that's now produced by S&P.

Bloomberg came out more recently with the UBS Bloomberg Constant Maturity Commodity Indexes (UBS Bloomberg CMCI), compiled for UBS AG. These indicators, unlike the others, adjust for changes in the time until contracts expire. Even

> **KEY POINT:**
>
> Indexes based on derivatives can be the underlying asset for other contracts.

173

so, they are similar in how they're organized and calculated.

Exhibit 12.1 tracks the performance of benchmark commodity indexes in the 2000s, when prices surged along with demand from China and elsewhere.

Compared with the other gauges, the UBS Bloomberg index fared the best because it didn't have any losses from selling futures as they expired and buying new ones.

The UBS Bloomberg indexes track 24 commodities, split into five categories: energy, precious

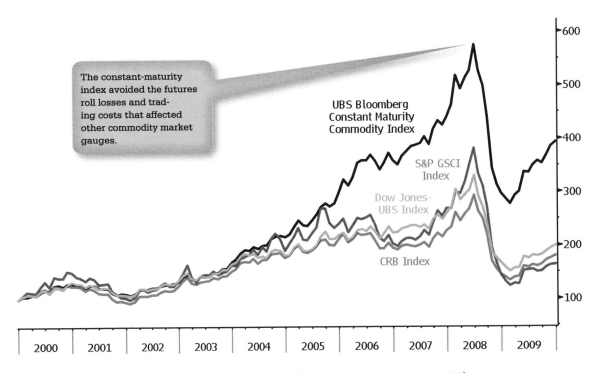

Exhibit 12.1: Commodity Index Total Returns (December 31, 1999 = 100)

metals, industrial metals, agriculture, and livestock. Each category has a separate series of gauges. Economic and trading indicators are used to determine a commodity's weight in the overall and category indexes.

Three types of constant maturity indicators are calculated. They start with price return indexes, which are based on changes in the value of commodity futures.

Excess return indexes add gains or losses from selling futures as they expire and buying contracts that mature later. This futures roll can add to returns when prices are lower in later months and reduce them when prices are higher.

Total return indexes add interest paid on the contract's margin, or money that the owner must keep on deposit. Treasury bill rates are used to calculate this component.

Other index providers use different commodities and categories, weighting criteria, and index names. Spot indexes are basically the same as the UBS Bloomberg price return indexes. They are calculated from futures prices rather than prices for immediate delivery.

Options

The prices paid for options show how much traders expect the value of the underlying asset to fluctuate, as mentioned earlier. With this in mind, derivatives exchanges and financial companies have created volatility indexes, which are tied to the value of several contracts.

The Chicago Board Options Exchange's Volatility Index (VIX) is the most widely followed of these indicators. This index is calculated from the prices of S&P 500 options, and it's designed to signal how much the index might swing within the next month. Futures, options, and exchange-traded securities are tied to its value.

There's a tendency for the VIX to rise when share prices are falling, and vice versa. Investors are more inclined to buy options to guard against further losses, or perhaps to speculate on rebounds, than they are to lock in gains as stocks climb. Because of this, the index is considered a gauge of investor fear.

The VIX was introduced in 1993, and the current version dates back to 2003. The CBOE switched to S&P 500 options from contracts on another index, the S&P 100, which had been more popular among derivatives traders. Exhibit 12.2 shows how the VIX fared during the "lost decade" of the 2000s.

The VIX peaked at 80.86 in November 2008, at the height of the U.S. financial crisis. Its low for the decade was 9.89, set in January 2007 as a five-year bull market in stocks neared its conclusion.

Bond, currency, and commodity indexes use options to gauge future volatility. Bank of America Corp.'s Merrill Lynch securities unit has the Merrill Option Volatility Estimate (MOVE) index. It's based on the value of contracts for two-year, five-year, and 10-year Treasury notes and 30-year bonds having one

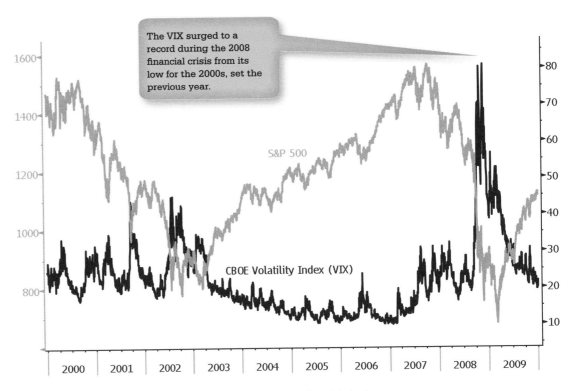

Exhibit 12.2: VIX Index versus Standard & Poor's 500 Index

month to maturity. JPMorgan Chase & Co. produces foreign-exchange volatility indexes for global markets, the Group of Seven industrial countries, and emerging markets. The CBOE provides crude oil and gold indexes, using options on funds that own the commodities.

Swaps

The CDS market is the place to look for swap-based indexes. Markit Group Ltd. calculates indexes for government and corporate CDS contracts that track the market and serve as the underlying asset for derivatives. Investors can buy index-based contracts to protect against or speculate on changes in government and corporate credit quality.

CDS indexes differ from other market gauges because time elements are built into them. Each index consists of contracts lasting for a specified period. Markit tracks swaps that last three years, seven years, and 10 years as well as five years, the industry benchmark. There's a maturity date as well. Corporate CDS indexes expire in June and December, in accordance with the terms of the contracts they track. They roll over in March and September.

Markit's SovX indexes follow the performance of sovereign CDS globally and regionally. Indicators are available for the world's investment-grade countries, Group of Seven countries, and emerging markets.

Another series of Markit indexes, known as CDX, are based on U.S. and Canadian corporate CDS. Barometers for investment-grade and high-yield debt protection are available. The CDX indexes cover emerging markets as well, and a separate series called iTraxx shows the performance of CDS for non-U.S. companies.

Funds

Individual investors can choose from thousands of open-end funds, closed-end funds, and exchange-traded mutual funds. Some of them are designed to surpass benchmark indexes, and others are

content to mirror them. Institutions have a similar bounty of choices in hedge funds as well as funds of funds.

How does anyone decide which funds to buy, sell, or hold? The answer often lies with performance. Funds that consistently produce larger gains or smaller losses than others in the same category are keepers. Funds that don't are sale candidates.

To determine how a fund and its manager are doing, it's possible to use market indexes. The S&P 500 would work for funds invested in the largest U.S. companies. Beating the S&P 500 may not be much of an accomplishment, though, if most funds in the category are doing the same.

That's where fund indexes come in handy. They provide a yardstick for measuring how well or poorly a fund and its manager are doing relative to their peers.

The Bloomberg Indexes for Active Funds are among the indicators, and they're worth a closer look. Peer groups are defined by three criteria: fund type, country of domicile, and Bloomberg objective. They're used to compile about 475 indexes for open-end funds, closed-end funds, exchange-traded funds (ETFs), hedge funds, and funds of funds.

Country of domicile refers to the location where the funds are registered. Many of them are based in the Cayman Islands and other places that provide tax advantages for investors. They are known as offshore funds and tracked separately from those based in the United States and elsewhere.

> **KEY POINT:**
> CDS indexes differ from bond indexes because they are linked to maturity dates. Bond market indicators drop securities as they mature and add new ones to take their place.

> **KEY POINT:**
> Indexes are a benchmark to judge how managers of active funds perform over time, and they are the basis for passive funds. Investors who beat their benchmark are said to generate alpha, or excess returns.

Bloomberg objectives are defined by funds' investments and strategy. Bond funds may focus on government debt, agency debt, corporate debt, municipal debt, or mortgage debt, or they may target high-yield securities. Stock funds may favor larger companies, smaller companies, or those in between. They may prefer to own the fastest growing companies, or the ones likely to offer the best value.

All these criteria are used to set objectives. With hedge funds, strategies come into play as well. There are macro indexes, long-biased and short-biased indexes, long-short indexes, market neutral indexes, arbitrage indexes, and managed futures indexes.

Lipper uses a similar approach for mutual fund indexes. Dow Jones and Credit Suisse AG jointly track the performance of hedge funds, and the indexes compete against gauges from Eurekahedge Pte, Hedge Fund Research Inc. and Hennessee Group. Cambridge Associates LLC and State Street Corp. are among the firms that produce indexes for private equity funds.

Bloomberg Functionality Cheat Sheet

Currencies

FXIP	FX information portal
FXTF	FX ticker finder
FXC	Currency rates matrix
WCR	World currency rates
WCRS	World currency ranker

Money Markets

PGM	Program lookup
MMR	Money rate monitors
BBAL	BBA Libor fixings
CPHS	Direct issuer CP rates
MMCV	Money-market curves

Government Bonds

BTMM	Treasury and money-market monitor
SOVM	Sovereign debt monitor
WB	World bond markets
GGR	Generic government rates
CRVF	Curve finder

Corporate Bonds

SECF	Security finder
NIM	New issue monitor for bonds
TRAC	TRACE home page
FICM	Fixed income credit monitor
YCRV	Yield curve analysis

Stocks

ECDR	Equity offerings
WEI	World equity indexes
MOST	Most active stocks
MOV	Index movers*
EQS	Equity screening

Commodities

SECF	Security finder
GLCO	Global commodity prices and data
NRG	Bloomberg Energy Service menu
MINE	Metals, minerals, and mining menu
AGRS	Agricultural markets menu

Real Estate

RE	Real estate menu
CRE	Commercial real estate data
RMEN	Global indexes
REUS	U.S. real estate
HSST	U.S. housing data

Futures

SECF	Security finder
CTM	Contract table menu
WEIF	World equity index futures
WBF	World bond futures
FRD	Currency spot and forward rates

Options

MOSO	Most active options
OMON	Option monitor*
CALL	Call option monitor*
PUT	Put option monitor*
OMST	Most active contracts*

Swaps

IRSB	Interest rate swap rates
WS	World swap matrix
USSW	U.S. swap market
CDS	Credit default swap overview
GCDS	Global CDS monitor

Funds

FUND	Funds and portfolio holdings
MHD	Mutual fund holdings*
EXTF	Exchange-traded products
HFND	Hedge fund home page
PE	Private equity home page

*Security-specific function

About the Author

David Wilson produces "Chart of the Day" stories for Bloomberg News that provide insight into U.S. markets, business, and the economy. He serves as stocks editor for Bloomberg Radio, where he reports, writes, and delivers hourly updates on market developments and analyst research. He is based in New York City.

Wilson joined Bloomberg News in 1990, when he became the second U.S. stock market reporter ever hired by the news service. He later ran the Princeton and New York bureaus, began a global training program for reporters and editors, wrote columns, and ran global stock market coverage. He co-wrote an edition of *The Bloomberg Way*, a guide to business and financial journalism, which was used worldwide for more than a decade.

Before coming to Bloomberg, Wilson worked for Dow Jones, where he rose from news assistant to stock reporter. His first market stories chronicled the aftermath of the market's Black Monday crash in 1987. He wrote for the Dow Jones News Service, and many of his stories appeared in the *Wall Street Journal*.

Wilson started his journalism career at the *Asbury Park Press*, where he was an editorial assistant and pop-music writer. He holds a bachelor's degree in English, with a concentration in media studies, from Monmouth University and an MBA degree from Rider University.

Index